Stir Crazy!

Also by Susan Jane Cheney
Breadtime Stories

Stir Crazy!

More than 100 Quick, Low-Fat Recipes
for Your Wok or Stir-Fry Pan

SUSAN JANE CHENEY
ILLUSTRATIONS BY NAVA ATLAS

CB
CONTEMPORARY BOOKS

Library of Congress Cataloging-in-Publication Data

Cheney, Susan Jane.
    Stir crazy! : more than 100 quick, low-fat recipes for your wok or stir-fry pan / Susan Jane Cheney ; illustrations by Nava Atlas.
       p.   cm.
    Includes index.
    ISBN 0-8092-3001-1
    1. Stir frying.   2. Wok cookery.   3. Quick and easy cookery.   4. Low-fat diet—Recipes.   I. Title.
TX689.5.C46   1997   97-33125
641.7'7—dc21   CIP

Featured on the cover: Curried Capellini (see page 113)

Cover design by Kim Bartko
Cover photograph © 1998 by Chris Cassidy
Interior design and illustrations by Nava Atlas

Published by Contemporary Books
A division of NTC/Contemporary Publishing Group, Inc.
4255 West Touhy Avenue, Lincolnwood (Chicago), Illinois 60646-1975 U.S.A.
Copyright © 1998 by Susan Jane Cheney
Illustrations copyright © 1998 by Nava Atlas
Printed in the United States of America
International Standard Book Number: 0-8092-3001-1
  15 14 13 12 11 10 9 8 7 6 5 4 3 2 1

With love and gratitude to David,
who's always eager for yet another culinary adventure

CONTENTS

ACKNOWLEDGMENTS

Many thanks to Nava Atlas for coming up with the idea for this project and contributing so handsomely to its personality and design. Thanks too to Patrice Connolly for finding the right publishing niche. Finally, thanks to Gerilee Hundt for her keen editorial expertise.

INTRODUCTION

Longing for great-tasting, wholesome meals, yet feeling frustrated by a hectic schedule that always seems to get in the way? Perhaps ironically, the answer to this ubiquitous modern dilemma might just be one of the oldest cooking tools known to humankind: a wok. Start with this venerable ancient Asian vessel or its contemporary counterpart, a large chef's or stir-fry pan; then add some fresh ingredients and an adventuresome spirit. Presto! You're ready to put supremely appealing and wholesome dishes together in a hurry, possibly with a bit of help from someone who's been "stir crazy" for quite a while now.

A big bowl-shaped pan offers today's health-conscious yet harried cooks exceptional versatility. Its generous capacity, concave shape, extensive surface area, and ready heat conductivity all add up to an extraordinarily efficient design. Stir-fries, the wok's signature products, may be the world's original "fast foods." Because their rapid cooking method requires little or no fat and locks in nutrients, stir-fries are especially healthful to boot. A wok is equally useful for braising, stewing, and steaming, all of which also result in quick, low-fat meals. Though chef's and stir-fry pans are sometimes smaller than the average home-sized wok, they're suitable for most of the same applications.

When woks became popular in the United States some 30 years ago, they were used exclusively for Asian-style dishes, certainly not everyday fare. The standard American evening meal consisted of a sizable serving of meat accompanied by several side dishes. Today's meals often consist of a single main dish or a congregation of several small ones. And Western tastes are increasingly daring, celebrating grains and vegetables and enthusiastically embracing the world's richly diverse cuisines. These changes offer exciting new roles for the wok, transforming it from a "once in a while" utensil to an all-purpose one.

Woks and wok-shaped pans are especially well suited to modern fast-paced lifestyles, meal concepts, and global culinary eclecticism. You'll find them equally effective for preparing Eastern European Paprika Noodles or a creamy Italian risotto as they are for Chinese lo mein or fried rice. International boundaries mean nothing to these enormously practical and adaptable pans.

Designed for hectic schedules, *Stir Crazy!* recipes are all easily prepared in a wok. They rely on the irresistible flavors of fresh vegetables, fruits, herbs, and spices combined with a pantry full of staples: grains, noodles, beans, nuts, seeds, oils, and seasonings. Among them are both new takes on traditional dishes and novel culinary creations. All are high in flavor, naturally low in fat, and meatless. Although developed as dairy-free, some recipes include dairy products as optional ingredients. Many stand alone as quickly prepared one-dish meals; others make satisfying snacks or complementary components of memorable feasts.

If you don't have a wok stored away in a kitchen cupboard and haven't acquired a stir-fry pan, turn to Chapter 1 before beginning your quest for the right one for you. Pan in hand, proceed to Chapter 2 for tips on cooking techniques, including stir-frying, braising, stewing, and steaming. This is a handy reference section to return to often. In Chapter 3, you'll start cooking—and keep it up through the next six.

"Vibrant Vegetables" showcases lively leafy greens, sweet compact roots, and everything in between in quickly cooked stir-fries or gently braised medleys. Try Coconut Mustard Greens or Gingery Kale and Crimson Cabbage for a salady side dish. Mushrooms Magnifique, Colorful Caponata, and several other selections make luscious light entrees.

"Savory Stews" offers an international collection of sumptuous simmered concoctions. If Moroccan Lentil Tangine doesn't match your mood on a given evening, go to Garlicky Garbanzos or Creamy Cauliflower and Carrot Curry.

"Tofu, Tempeh, and Seitan Specialties" takes these three tremendously versatile age-old Asian foods and gives them contemporary tastes. I think you'll be delightfully surprised by such dishes as Tofu and Green Tomato Stir-Fry, Tempeh Mushroom Marsala, and Seitan Tzimmes.

"Grains Galore" gathers up grains from different corners of the world and adapts them to appetites in every season, from spring-infused Risotto Primavera to warming Cool-Season Couscous.

"Oodles of Noodles" seeks inspiration for innovative noodle dishes from some of the world's greatest cuisines, from the Far East to the Mediterranean. Farfalle with Fennel and Arugula, Broccoli-Almond Udon, and Corn Twists with Collards and Black-Eyed Peas are but a small sampling.

"Simple Sauces and Classy Condiments" amply demonstrates a wok's special suitability for preparing toppings and relishes. You may be amazed at how easy it is to simmer Gingered Tomato Chutney, Good Gravy, Nectarine Ketchup, and other sauces and such in a round-bottomed "saucepan."

Last, "It's a Wrap" taps into the well-established worldwide trend to enclose anything and everything in various types of bread for eating out of hand. Dishes like Mushroom-Stuffed Steamed Buns, Seitan Fakin' Fajitas, and Chock-Full Chapatis show you how to convert your stir-fry pan into a creative "sandwich" maker.

Keep in mind as you use the book that there's plenty of room for flexibility and improvisation to accommodate the contents of your pantry on any given day and your own particular taste. If I call for leeks and you have only onions, don't hesitate to substitute. Just think flavor families and similar textures. I'm a confirmed garlic lover, and you'll find this reflected in most recipes, but feel free to adjust garlic amounts to your own liking. Also, I've gone rather easy on oil throughout the book. If you prefer richer flavors and don't mind the extra fat, add a bit more. By the way, be sure to pay attention to the smoke point as well as flavors of the oils you choose to use. High-heat cooking requires an oil with a high smoke point to prevent the oil and consequent taste and healthfulness of the dish from breaking down. In certain recipes I have turned down the heat to match the oil I wanted to use; you can turn it back up if you select a more heat-stable oil.

Vegetable stock appears in many recipes, and it's easy and economical to make yourself. You will avoid the excess salt and monosodium glutamate often added to commercial stocks, and you can customize the flavor for particular preparations. Just keep a quart-sized plastic container in your freezer and gradually fill it with vegetable odds and ends and parings. Include carrot, parsnip, sweet or white potato, summer and winter squashes, shiitake mushroom stems, fennel, celery, corncobs, anything in the onion family, parsley stems, perhaps a bay leaf or a bit of apple or pear. When it's full, combine the contents with two to three quarts of water and simmer covered for an hour or so, then strain, cool, and refrigerate or freeze. Avoid peppers, eggplant, and cruciferous vegetables like cabbage, mustard, kale, collards, broccoli, cauliflower, kohlrabi, brussels sprouts, turnips, watercress, rutabagas, and radishes in your stock, or you may end up with a strong-flavored, bitter brew. Add special tastes, say tomatoes, beets, ginger, or fresh herbs, if you have a particular dish in mind. When I specify "vegetable stock" in recipes, I'm always referring to unsalted stock.

A few ingredients in recipes may be unfamiliar to you. Though some of these are native to the Far East, their application is not limited to Asian cuisines. For instance, I favor powdered kuzu (spelled *kudzu* in the United States) for thickening purposes because of the unsurpassed smooth texture it produces, its tastelessness, and its inherent medicinal qualities. Substitute arrowroot powder if you prefer. Both of these natural, minimally processed roots are preferable to highly refined cornstarch, which often gives sauces an elastic quality and a raw starchy taste. Miso is another favorite product that originated in the East. Used for seasoning, this fermented soybean paste adds a wonderful depth of flavor to a wide range of preparations. Moreover, you'll find a variety of misos to introduce subtle flavor differences and add interest to dishes. Check the glossary at the end of this book for other definitions and explanations.

To use the book most effectively, I suggest you peruse the first two chapters for fundamentals before turning to the recipes. Then read a recipe thoroughly before beginning a dish. By the way, I've economized on words: in recipes, read "wok" as "wok or stir-fry pan." Now, get out your wok—or stir-fry pan—gather your ingredients, and go stir crazy!

1
Selecting a Pan and Accessories

First things first: if you don't already have one, how do you choose a wok or its modern equivalent from today's broad selection? And which other implements are really necessary accessories? This chapter will guide your search for new tools and help you care for your pans, both new and old.

Choosing a Pan

If you're shopping for a new pan, you'll have a number of choices. Take a tour of Asian markets, specialty cookware shops, and department stores to see what's available. Woks and contemporary woklike pans come in different sizes, materials, and even shapes. Make your decision based on how you're most likely to use your pan, subject, of course, to budget constraints and aesthetic preferences.

Though woks come larger and smaller, a 14-inch-diameter one is most manageable and practical for home use. It fits on a standard home stove burner and inside a typical kitchen sink for cleaning. A pan this size will accommodate four to six servings of food, but you can also easily prepare less if you're feeding just one or two. Most stir-fry or chef's pans, though they have the same bowl shape as a wok, are no larger than 12 inches in diameter.

You may find woks wrought from carbon steel, stainless steel, cast iron, tempered iron, or aluminum, and you'll likely come across electric woks, too. Most stir-fry pans are composed of stainless steel or aluminum. Each material has its distinct advantages and drawbacks, and a pan's price tag will basically reflect the material it's composed of and processes required to produce it.

My first wok, an inexpensive Asian import composed of tempered iron, is still going strong after 25 years. The ubiquitous wok of that earlier time, this veteran is durable, relatively lightweight, and easy to manipulate. It's an excellent heat conductor that responds rapidly to temperature adjustments. Domestically produced spun-carbon-steel woks seem to have supplanted tempered-iron ones but closely resemble them physically and functionally; they're also comparably priced. You'll need to season carbon steel and iron woks before their first use to prevent rust and off-tastes from acidic ingredients, such as tomatoes, citrus fruits, wine, and vinegar.

Cast-iron woks also require seasoning unless they have an enamel surface coating. These hefty pans conduct heat well and evenly, though they take longer than thinner iron or steel pans to heat up and cool down. It's advisable to bring a cast-iron wok to a high temperature over medium heat. Once the pan has heated, it will remain hot at an even lower setting. Because of their weight, cast-iron woks are somewhat awkward to handle on and off the stove and in the sink.

Stainless steel doesn't conduct, retain, or distribute heat as well as either carbon steel or iron. If you decide on a stainless-steel wok or stir-fry pan, select one with a multi-ply aluminum or copper core that not only covers the bottom but goes all the way up the sides. Multilayered pans are considerably more expensive but well worth the extra investment, since foods tend to burn quite easily in single-ply stainless steel, especially when set above medium heat. A stainless-steel pan excels especially at stewing and steaming because prolonged contact with water and moist ingredients doesn't harm its surface in the least.

Aluminum pans heat quickly and maintain a consistent temperature during cooking. This lightweight metal, however, reacts with acidic foods, discoloring them and adversely affecting their taste. If you're interested in an aluminum pan, look into hard-anodized cookware. A pan of this material begins as a heavy-gauge flat aluminum disk. As with carbon steel, it's then formed into a bowl shape by spinning or drawing, processes that create a uniform quality in the metal, preventing the hot spots that sometimes occur in cast cookware. Next the pan undergoes hard anodization, a multistage electrochemical procedure that changes the molecular structure of its surface, making it denser, nonporous, abrasion resistant, and nonreactive. Hard-anodized pans have a naturally stick-resistant surface that doesn't require seasoning and isn't marred by metal utensils. These are more expensive than spun-steel pans but considerably less costly than high-quality multi-ply stainless steel.

Portability and freeing up stovetop space are electric woks' main pluses. But despite temperature controls, some cannot reach or maintain a heat high enough for successful stir-frying. Look for one with no less than 1,500 watts of power. Because of an electric wok's built-in heat source, it's especially crucial to remove cooked food expeditiously, before it gets overdone. And unless an electric wok has a removable heat control unit, it's a chore to clean.

Whatever material they're made of, some woks and stir-fry pans have nonstick surface coatings that allow fat-free cooking and are especially easy to clean. Coated surfaces' biggest disadvantage is their potential for chipping, scratching, and peeling. In general, none stand up as well to high heat as a seasoned steel or iron surface, but some do better than others, depending on the specific coating. Manufacturers usually advise using wooden, plastic, or rubber utensils in a coated pan to protect its surface.

When you've decided on composition, consider pan shape. Round-bottomed woks are traditional, originally designed to rest in a circular opening in the top of ancient Asian stoves. There they were directly above or surrounded by the fire and remained stable during vigorous stirring. Round-bottomed woks' inherent tippiness is a problem on modern flat-burnered range tops, though a ring stand readily resolves instability for the most part, and the advantages of a round bottom outweigh this small inconvenience. A concave surface is ideal for stirring sauces, and it makes cooking small quantities particularly easy. Also, cooking in a round-bottomed wok requires less oil than is necessary in a flat-bottomed pan.

Flat-bottomed woks resemble high-sided skillets. These are the wisest way to go when you're cooking on an electric stove, because the burners have insufficient contact with a round-bottomed pan to heat it adequately. Electric ranges are frustrating for wok cooking in general because they respond slowly to temperature adjustments. The most effective technique is to set a burner on its highest temperature and then move the pan on and off it to modulate the heat level. One asset of a flat-bottomed pan is its stability.

For convenience and safety, good-sized woks and stir-fry pans should have securely fastened handles on both sides. These are often identical metal loops, though some pans have a long handle on one side and a helper handle on the other. Wooden handles will protect you from burns, though they are susceptible to scorching during high-heat cooking.

Woks and wok-style pans are so useful, you may want more than one. It's handy to have a well-seasoned carbon steel, tempered-iron, or cast-iron pan for stir-frying and other fat-based cooking and a stainless-steel one for steaming and stewing. If you're a one-pan person, a hard-anodized aluminum wok may be the best all-purpose selection.

Useful Accessories

I've already described the value of a ring stand for stabilizing a round-bottomed wok. Some of these metal collars, as they're also called, have tapered sides that allow you to set a wok closer or farther from the heat by simply turning the stand over. You may prefer to dispense with the stand and set your wok directly on a gas burner for high-heat stir-frying. Use the more stable stand for braising, stewing, and steaming at more moderate heats.

You'll want a wok lid to allow for steaming. Most are aluminum rounded or flat-topped domes. The more room a lid leaves inside the wok, the better. High bell-shaped covers provide adequate space when you're steaming something on a rack inside the wok.

A long-handled shovel-shaped Chinese-style stirring implement is particularly effective for wok cooking. It has a thin broad blade with a curved front edge and slightly raised sides. You'll find these in both stainless and carbon steel. Look for one with a bamboo or wooden grip to protect your hand. Thin-bladed wooden paddles are other effective stirring utensils.

Finally, a rack is essential for steaming, and I'll talk more about this in Chapter 2. Woks often come in sets with some or all of the preceding items. You can also purchase accessories separately.

Seasoning and Cleaning Your Pan

Uncoated carbon-steel and iron woks require seasoning before they are used. When you season a wok, you're creating a somewhat nonstick surface coating that seals the metal pores, preventing rust. First scrub the surface well with hot, soapy water to remove any preservative oil applied by the manufacturer. Dry the wok thoroughly by placing it over low heat. Using a paper towel, rub the entire inner surface with a light layer of cooking oil. Heat the wok until the oil just begins to smoke and the inside turns golden brown. Repeat this process several times. Seasoning will progress as you cook in your wok, and it will darken with further use. Should a patch of rust appear, scour the area with fine steel wool and season it again.

A well-seasoned wok rarely requires more than gentle scrubbing with hot water. A bamboo brush is a good tool for removing cooked-on food particles from the surface without jeopardizing its protective coat. Rub some salt onto the dry burned surface first if you're dealing with an especially tough situation. Avoid soap as much as possible and abrasive scouring pads altogether. Always dry your clean seasoned wok completely after rinsing. Brush the inside with a little cooking oil and place it over medium heat for 15 to 30 seconds. Cool and wipe off any remaining oil before storing. Keep your wok in a well-ventilated spot and use it frequently to prevent oil on the surface from turning rancid.

2

Streamlining Stir-Frying Plus Other Techniques and Tips

A wok is a somewhat exotic-looking pan, but cooking in it is a straightforward proposition. The same goes for stir-fry pans modeled on their proven predecessors. Wok means simply "pot" in Chinese, and it occupies the same all-purpose status in many other Asian countries. Adopt a broad-minded view of this remarkably versatile vessel rather than think of it as a specialized utensil for Asian-style meals. Regard your wok or stir-fry pan as a large skillet, saucepan, stew or soup pot, and steamer all rolled into one, useful for preparing practically any type of cuisine.

A wok's unique design offers numerous advantages to cooks. Its generous capacity and depth permit energetic stirring while keeping ingredients confined. Though hottest on the bottom, its widely flared sides distribute the heat, maximizing the available cooking surface. Finally, a wok's big bowl shape is especially easy to scoop food out of for serving.

For best results from your wok, study the following sections on specific cooking techniques. From stir-frying to steaming, they offer tips on taking full advantage of your pan's exceptionally adaptable character. Let's start with a wok's most notorious application: stir-frying.

STIR-FRYING

Rapidly cooking chopped food by keeping it in constant motion over high heat, stir-frying undoubtedly developed as a way to conserve fuel. It's similar to French sautéing but even faster. Besides economizing on time, stir-frying produces healthful and aesthetically appealing results by sealing in nutrients, natural juices, and flavor and preserving ingredients' colors and textures. This method requires minimal oil because only a small portion of the ingredients cook in it at any given moment: As soon as an item is seared, it's pushed up the side, out of the hot heart of the pan.

Stir-frying on a standard residential range is somewhat of a compromise. Commercial establishments benefit from larger, hotter burners designed for rapid cooking and conservation of vegetables' colors and textures. Yet wonderful results can be produced on a residential range; attention to details can make a huge difference when stir-frying at home.

Stir-frying demands quick actions and judgments and therefore requires smooth coordination, a good sense of timing, and concentration. The goal is to cook each ingredient just the right amount to elicit its own special contribution to the ensemble—no easy trick! Remember that cooking times will vary with pan composition and heat intensity, determined in part by how close your pan is to the flame. You will eventually get to know your particular pan and learn about the character of each ingredient so that everything ends up done at once. Don't worry if you feel flustered in your first stir-frying attempts. Practice makes perfect, and there are ways to streamline the process.

Get Ready

Preparation and organization are prime prerequisites because you won't have time to rummage in the cabinet for a forgotten ingredient or chop another vegetable in the midst of stir-frying. Soak any dried mushrooms and other dehydrated vegetables and marinate ingredients ahead of time. Combine liquids that you'll be adding to the stir-fry together. Do the same with any dry seasonings. If a recipe requires a sauce, mix it up and dissolve any thickeners before beginning to cook.

Dry all fresh vegetables well, because extra moisture will cause the oil to spatter and lower the heat in the wok. Slice vegetables uniformly in both size and shape. Similarly sized pieces will take approximately the same amount of time to cook, provided the vegetables are of equal hardness. Making vegetables the same shape also lends an aesthetic touch: if you're including green beans, for instance, slice red bell pepper and golden zucchini into thin strips about the same length as the beans. For stir-frying it's definitely preferable to cut vegetables into small pieces designed for quick cooking.

Roll cutting is one of my favorite techniques for carrots and other long cylindrical vegetables. Start by holding the vegetable with its narrow tip pointing away from you. Cut it at an angle with a chef's knife or cleaver, then give the vegetable about a quarter-turn and cut another slice at the same angle as before. Continue turning and slicing until you have the amount you need.

Several other cutting techniques are useful. For graceful thin slices, cut large-diameter vegetables into long pieces before slicing them on a diagonal. Shredding—really slivering, also described as julienne or matchsticks—is another way to produce fine slices: cut the item into thin slabs and then into delicate strips. To dice, slice a food lengthwise the thickness you want your cubes to be, cut long strips at even intervals, then pile up the strips and cut across them to form cubes. Use the same technique for mincing, really a tiny dice; continue chopping until you achieve the desired fineness.

Some vegetables don't require cutting at all. Break broccoli and cauliflower into fine florets. Small mushrooms can be used whole, or slice them into halves or quarters if slightly larger.

Get Set

Now it's time to get organized and thoroughly think through the cooking process. Group cut vegetables in separate piles on a platter or in individual bowls. Put together all the hard vegetables, carrots, turnips, and cauliflower for example, followed by softer ones such as mushrooms and summer squash, then the quickest-cooking items like greens, sprouts, and fresh herbs.

By the way, just about any vegetable is suitable for stir-frying. Don't limit your choices to "Oriental" ingredients: it's the technique, not necessarily every aspect of its native cuisine, that you're after. Choose a combination based on coordinated colors, textures, and flavors. Just be sure to analyze each vegetable's characteristics to determine how best to prepare it and when to add it.

Assemble the vegetables, along with all other ingredients and utensils you'll need while cooking—oil, condiments, liquids, stirring spatula, pot holders, wok lid, and any garnishes—within easy reach of the cooking surface. You may want to arrange everything in order of use.

Go!

Now you're ready for action. Recipes give specific directions, but most follow certain basic steps. Let's go through a generic stir-fry just to help you get the hang of this cooking process.

Set your dry wok on a burner and heat it until a drop of water sizzles and evaporates as soon as it hits the surface. Pour in the oil and swirl it to coat the sides of the pan. The oil will warm quickly; it should bubble but not smoke. As my first Chinese cooking teacher used to say: "Hot pan, warm oil." Use just enough oil to keep the ingredients from sticking.

Select oils for stir-frying carefully. Not all oils are appropriate for high-heat cooking. Use smoke point as a major criterion. Generally, refined oils have more heat tolerance than unrefined ones, but choose high-quality refined oils in the interest of good health. Avocado and almond oils have especially high smoke points. Refined peanut, sesame, high-oleic safflower and sunflower, and canola oils are also appropriate for high-heat cooking. Reserve unrefined oils, including extra-virgin olive oil, for medium to medium-high heat and take care that they do not smoke. I always use organic cold-pressed extra-virgin olive oil. You can combine oils for the best of both worlds—heat tolerance and flavor. Canolive, a combination of canola and olive oils, is a popular commercial blend. Add a bit of unrefined sesame, walnut, or other flavorful oil to an oil with a high smoke point to enhance the taste of a dish. Avoid corn oil for frying, because it tends to foam.

It's possible to stir-fry without any oil at all, using a flavorful vegetable broth, wine, or some other liquid. Heat the liquid to bubbling before adding any other ingredients and keep it hot while stir-frying. The liquid will mostly or entirely cook away during the cooking process.

After you've added the oil (or broth), immediately add onions if you're including them. Stir constantly with one hand and add ingredients with the other. Continuous movement is necessary to ensure that all the raw pieces have sufficient contact with the bottom of the pan yet don't burn. Other pungent seasonings you're using to flavor the entire dish such as garlic, fresh ginger, and hot chiles customarily are added at the beginning of cooking, but I find that when included too early these tend to burn and taste bitter. I usually add garlic soon after the onions but often wait on ginger and chiles until a bit later. For a subtle seasoning effect, add thick slices of garlic and ginger or whole chiles first but then remove them with a slotted spoon after their flavors have permeated the oil.

As soon as the seasonings become aromatic, add vegetables, beginning with those that are hardest and thus take longest to cook—carrots and other root vegetables, for example. Keep stirring energetically but carefully, constantly lifting and turning the ingredients. Add about a handful of vegetables at a time to avoid reducing the temperature of the pan. As these vegetables cook, push them up the sides of the wok. Then progress to softer vegetables. Keep the oil hot enough to sear the vegetables and lock in their juices. Stir-frying takes minutes—sometimes seconds, depending on the ingredient. Don't overload the wok; 5 cups of vegetables is just about the upper limit for a single successful stir-fry. Greens are an exception, because they cook down so dramatically. Make a second batch if you're cooking in quantity and be sure to reheat the pan adequately between batches.

Next add any stock and liquid seasonings such as soy sauce, sherry, or vinegar. Pour liquids around the inside of the rim so they'll heat as they run down the sides of the pan. You may need to cover the wok at this point to allow firmer vegetables to steam briefly and cook through. Wait until after you've finished steaming to add tender greens, such as spinach, to preserve their bright color.

Add a thickener last. Push the vegetables up the side of the wok and pour the dissolved thickener into the hot liquid on the bottom. Stir until the liquid is thick and smooth.

Stop Cooking but Keep Going!

Remove the wok from the heat, taste, and adjust seasonings if necessary. At this point it's important to keep up your momentum and move quickly. To serve the freshest, crispest final product, it's best to have plates at hand (I usually warm them slightly in the oven ahead of time) and diners already seated at the table. Quickly line the plates with warm rice, another grain, or noodles, top it with some of the stir-fry, and pass them around immediately. Transfer any stir-fry remaining in the pan to another bowl to prevent it from continuing to cook in the hot pan and quickly becoming overdone.

Refrigerate leftover stir-fry. Although never as dazzling the next day, it makes a great stuffing to roll up in a warmed flat bread for a quick meal. Or use it as a head start on a quick soup: Combine the leftover stir-fried vegetables with hot vegetable stock or miso broth and some cooked noodles, and you've created an easy nourishing lunch—or breakfast. "Soupy noodles" is one of my family's favorite waker-uppers.

BRAISING

This is a two-step cooking process that begins with browning in hot oil followed by gentle simmering in a relatively small amount of added liquid in a covered pan. Certain vegetables, such as eggplant, celery, fennel, onions, carrots, and other roots, take especially well to this cooking technique and are often showcased alone or in simple combinations. Some vegetables are braised whole, others in various-sized pieces, usually larger than those for stir-fries.

The chosen liquid, say a tasty vegetable stock, can contribute considerably to a braise. Wine, fruit juices, and other acidic liquids help soft vegetables retain some structural integrity as they're braised. Liquid reduces during braising, and any that remains at the end usually has a glazed, saucelike consistency.

If you're using a carbon-steel or cast-iron pan for braising—or the next technique, stewing—be sure it's well seasoned. Otherwise it's likely to rust, and acidic vegetables and liquids may cause a metallic taste and discoloration.

STEWING

Stewing is slow simmering, usually in a covered pan. In many cases it begins with a bit of sautéing or stir-frying up front, which makes it quite similar to braising, though stews are generally more complex concoctions and consequently feature a longer list of ingredients. Still, the objective of stewing is the same as braising: to soften the ingredients and marry their flavors.

Unlike most braises, the liquid in stews often is released by the ingredients themselves. In Provençal Summer Stew, for instance, the majority of the liquid comes from the tomatoes. If too much liquid remains when the vegetables reach a desirable texture, it may be necessary to simmer the stew uncovered to reduce the excess to a saucelike consistency. Stews composed of all firm, less juicy vegetables do require some added liquid.

Vegetables in stews are usually diced or sliced larger than for stir-fries. It's generally best to add these gradually, in order of their hardness or cooking time. As with stir-fries, add fresh herbs and greens just before serving to preserve their bright colors and tastes.

STEAMING

Steaming cooks foods in the moist hot air over boiling water. Steamed vegetables retain their vivid colors, vital flavors, and pleasing textures, so long as they're not overcooked. Chinese-style steamed buns and dumplings have a wonderful moistness, entirely unlike similar items cooked with dry heat. You can even steam breads, cakes, and puddings in tightly covered containers.

A bamboo steamer is an Asian tradition. It consists of one to several stacked trays with a rounded cover and sits over boiling water inside a wok. Tiered racks allow steaming on several different levels simultaneously. The latticework bamboo or rattan racks permit steam to escape without condensing and bathing the steaming food. But a simple perforated metal rack or a round wire cooling rack combined with a wok lid will suffice as a steamer.

Fill the wok with water to just about an inch below the rack. Arrange items to be steamed in a single layer on the rack. I put buns on small squares of baking parchment to prevent sticking. Line bamboo steaming trays with a slightly damp cloth to absorb excess steam and prevent small items from falling through. Place anything that will give up much juice on a heatproof plate on the rack; there should be at least a 1-inch space all around between the plate and the side of the steamer or wok to permit steam to circulate freely. Heat the water just to boiling, then cover the steamer or wok tightly and reduce the heat to maintain a gentle simmer.

Occasionally check to be sure the water doesn't evaporate away during steaming. When you remove the lid, take care that escaping steam doesn't burn your hands. Rubber gloves or an oven mitt is a good precaution. If the water level is low, add boiling water so as not to suspend the steaming process.

Steaming is relatively quick, and it's best not to overestimate cooking time. Check on steamed items before you think they'll be done; you can always steam them a bit longer if necessary.

Another wok cooking process often referred to as *steaming* occurs when some liquid is added during or at the end of stir-frying and the wok is covered for several minutes to finish cooking harder vegetables. To forgo this step, you can steam or blanch hard vegetables before stir-frying.

3

VIBRANT VEGETABLES

Most of us associate woks with colorful, crisp vegetable stir-fries, and this cooking vessel unquestionably excels at preserving tender vegetables' bright hues, appealing crunchy textures, and valuable nutrients. Quick vegetable stir-fries require little preparation and provide almost immediate gratification. Light braising and steaming are other wok cooking fortes, especially effective with denser vegetables such as roots and tubers.

There's an enormous assortment of ingredients to choose from throughout the year, and I find that some of the simplest, most straightforward presentations of seasonal vegetables win out over elaborate combinations. A few well-chosen complementary flavors in Zucchini with Zip, for instance, let the pure essence of this summer superstar shine through. Modest amounts of garlic and nutmeg neatly knit together the individual tastes of white potatoes and yams in One Potato, Two Potato. In Brussels Sprouts with Pears and Hazelnuts, fruit and nuts transform brussels sprouts from unpretentious peasants to elegant sophisticates, welcome on any holiday table.

Quick-cooked greens are an agreeable alternative to raw salads, especially in cold weather. You'll likely discover that piquant Wilted "Mustard" Greens is a universal palate pleaser, and Super-Quick Spinach with Pine Nuts complements most any Mediterranean main dish you might serve; both take moments to toss together.

While most of the dishes in this chapter are intended as side dishes, a combination of two or three easily suffices for a light dinner. Some will also stand alone as entrees when paired with pasta or a grain. Supper's a cinch when you serve Simple Sweet and Sour Cabbage over any short cut of pasta, Rainbow Peppers and Red Onion with grilled polenta, or Summer Sisters Stir-Fry over quinoa.

Thai Asparagus Treat

Tender asparagus shoots are a welcome sign of spring, and Thai seasonings provide a wonderful way to enjoy them. Peel the lower part of the stalks before slicing if the skin is thick and tough.

1 tablespoon peanut oil
4 large scallions, sliced thin
2 teaspoons grated peeled fresh ginger
2 tablespoons thinly sliced fresh lemongrass
Minced or ground dried red chiles to taste
1 pound asparagus, sliced on a diagonal,
    stalks and tips kept separate
3 to 4 tablespoons vegetable stock or water
1 tablespoon fresh lime juice
1 tablespoon shoyu or natural soy sauce
2 tablespoons minced fresh mint
¼ cup chopped fresh cilantro
Salt to taste

Set a wok over high heat. Add the oil and swirl it to coat the inside of the pan. Add the scallions and stir-fry briefly. Add the ginger, lemongrass, and chiles and continue stir-frying, gradually adding the asparagus, sliced stalks first. Add stock, a tablespoon at a time, and stir-fry until the asparagus is tender but still bright green. Add the lime juice, shoyu, mint, and fresh cilantro. Toss well. Taste and add salt if needed. Serve immediately.

Serves 4

Calories: 63   Total fat: 4 g   Protein: 2 g
Carbohydrates: 6 g   Cholesterol: 0 g   Sodium: 262 mg

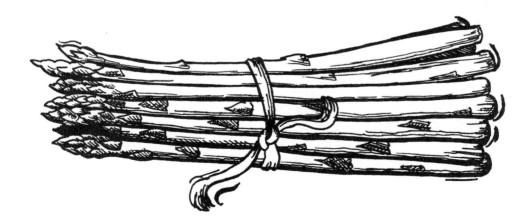

Sweet Winter Roots

Simmering in sweet cider gives these rather pungent vegetables a luscious, mellow flavor and tender, somewhat glazed texture. Cook carrots and parsnips this way too—separately, together, or combined with turnips and/or rutabagas.

1 tablespoon light sesame oil
1 medium onion, sliced lengthwise into
*   crescents*
1½ cups 2-inch-long turnip strips
1½ cups rutabaga, cut to match turnip
¾ teaspoon grated peeled fresh ginger
¾ cup apple cider or unsweetened apple
*   juice*
Freshly ground black pepper to taste
Salt to taste

Set a wok over medium-high heat. Add the oil and swirl it to coat the inside of the pan. Add the onion and stir-fry for 3 to 4 minutes, until it softens and appears translucent. Gradually add the turnip and rutabaga and continue to stir-fry for 3 to 4 minutes.

Stir in the ginger and cider. Bring the liquid to a simmer. Reduce the heat, cover the wok, and cook, stirring occasionally, for 10 to 15 minutes, until the vegetables are tender and the liquid has almost cooked away. Add black pepper and salt to taste.

Serves 4

Variation: Season the vegetables with a bit of cinnamon, nutmeg, cloves, or other sweet spices instead of—or in addition to—the fresh ginger.

Calories: 105   Total fat: 3 g   Protein: 1 g
Carbohydrates: 17 g   Cholesterol: 0 g   Sodium: 310 mg

Coconut Mustard Greens

Stir-frying tones down the inherent hotness of the mustard greens, while coconut and lime contribute a slightly exotic flavor twist; red radish adds contrasting color and crunch. Pair this with curries and other spicy dishes.

2 teaspoons peanut oil
½ to 1 cup thinly sliced mustard green stalks
4 cups firmly packed finely chopped mustard greens, stalks trimmed
6 to 8 medium red radishes, cut into thin slivers
4 large scallions, chopped fine
½ cup finely grated fresh coconut
2 teaspoons fresh lime juice
Salt to taste

Set a wok over medium to high heat. Add the oil and swirl it to coat the inside of the pan. Add the mustard green stalks and stir-fry for about 1 minute. Gradually add the mustard greens and radishes, stirring constantly. After a minute or two, when the greens are wilted but just tender and still bright green, stir in the scallions and coconut.

Remove the wok from the heat and stir in the lime juice. Season with salt.

Serves 4

Calories: 157	Total fat: 13 g	Protein: 2 g
Carbohydrates: 7 g	Cholesterol: 0 g	Sodium: 25 mg

Gingery Kale and Crimson Cabbage

Stir-fried kale and red cabbage make a tasty, colorful addition to many meals. Fresh ginger contributes its lively charm. Kale varies considerably in tenderness, depending on the variety and season. You may require extra liquid and brief steaming to tenderize the tough sort.

1 bunch (about ½ pound) kale
1 tablespoon light sesame oil
1 cup thinly sliced well-rinsed leek
1 teaspoon grated peeled fresh ginger
2 cups thinly sliced red cabbage
2 to 3 tablespoons vegetable stock or water
    or as needed
Umeboshi vinegar or salt to taste

Strip the leafy part of the kale off the stems with a sharp knife, then finely chop the stems and leaves separately.

Set a wok over medium-high heat, then add the oil and swirl it to coat the inside of the pan. Add the leek and stir-fry for about 1 minute. Stir in the kale stems and continue to stir-fry another minute or so, until almost tender. Add the ginger and cabbage, then gradually add the kale leaves and stir-fry several minutes longer, until the kale is just tender. If the wok becomes dry, add stock or water, cover the pan, and steam briefly. Season with umeboshi vinegar or salt and serve immediately.

Serves 4

Calories: 85   Total fat: 3 g   Protein: 2 g
Carbohydrates: 11 g   Cholesterol: 0 g   Sodium: 34 mg

Spicy Pakistani Potatoes and Cauliflower

Serve this Pakistani-style vegetable dish with long-grain rice or flat bread.

2 to 3 teaspoons light sesame oil
1 medium onion, chopped fine
2 teaspoons minced garlic
1 teaspoon grated peeled fresh ginger
1 small cauliflower, cut into bite-sized
    florets and stems
1 large potato, peeled if desired, and diced
    fine
Freshly ground black pepper to taste
1 teaspoon ground cumin
Pinch of ground cardamom
Pinch of ground cloves
¼ cup vegetable stock
Salt to taste
¼ cup chopped fresh cilantro

Set a wok over medium-high heat. Add 2 teaspoons of the oil and swirl it to coat the sides. Add the onion and stir-fry for 2 to 3 minutes, until it appears translucent. Stir in the garlic and ginger and continue stir-frying for several minutes, gradually adding the cauliflower and potato. Add another teaspoon of oil if the vegetables are sticking. Add the pepper, cumin, cardamom, and cloves and stir-fry for about 1 minute longer.

Add the vegetable stock and bring it to a simmer. Cover the wok, reduce the heat to low, and cook for 5 to 10 minutes, until the vegetables are very tender and the flavors melded. If too much liquid remains, continue to cook uncovered for several minutes more. Mash slightly if desired and season with salt to taste. Stir in the cilantro just before serving.

Serves 4

Calories: 147
Carbohydrates: 28 g
Total fat: 2 g
Cholesterol: 0 g
Protein: 2 g
Sodium: 32 mg

Super-Quick Spinach with Pine Nuts

*S*erve this as a side dish with your next Mediterranean meal.

4 teaspoons extra-virgin olive oil
4 large cloves garlic, minced or sliced thin
1 pound well-rinsed coarsely chopped
    spinach leaves
4 teaspoons fresh lemon juice
Freshly ground black pepper to taste
Salt to taste
2 tablespoons lightly toasted pine nuts

Set a wok over medium-high heat. Pour the oil around the rim and tilt the pan to coat the sides. Add the garlic and stir-fry for about 1 minute, taking care not to burn it. Add the spinach and continue to stir-fry briefly, just until wilted but still bright green. Remove the wok from the heat and add the lemon juice, pepper, and salt. Serve immediately, garnished with the pine nuts.

Serves 4

Calories: 95   Total fat: 6 g   Protein: 3 g
Carbohydrates: 5 g Cholesterol: 0 g   Sodium: 90 mg

Wilted "Mustard" Greens

Combine any collection of tender young leafy greens for this dish: kale, beet, mustard, dandelion, turnip, spinach, chard, radicchio, arugula, endive, escarole, and others. Some supermarkets now carry a "braising mixture" that's perfect. Experiment with different oils, vinegars, and mustards to modulate the flavor.

2 tablespoons prepared stone-ground
    mustard
2 tablespoons apple cider vinegar
1 tablespoon extra-virgin olive oil
4 scallions, sliced thin
4 to 6 cloves garlic, minced
1 pound well-rinsed, coarsely chopped
    mixed greens
Freshly ground black pepper to taste
Salt to taste
2 to 4 tablespoons chopped pitted kalamata
    olives (optional)

Whisk together the mustard and vinegar; set aside.

Set a wok over medium-high heat. Pour in the oil and swirl it to coat the sides of the pan. Add the scallions and garlic; stir-fry for about 1 minute. Gradually add the greens, stir-frying until they wilt but are still colorful. Stir in the mustard and vinegar mixture and season with pepper and salt. Stir in the olives if desired.

Serves 4

Calories: 108   Total fat: 4 g   Protein: 3 g
Carbohydrates: 12 g   Cholesterol: 0 g   Sodium: 261 mg

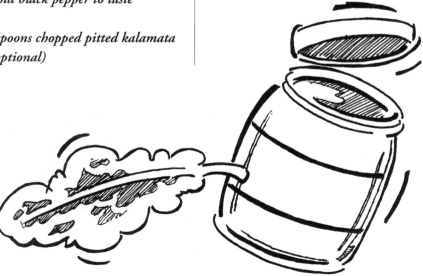

Mushrooms Magnifique

Try this simple yet elegant stir-fry over nutty-flavored basmati rice.

4 teaspoons extra-virgin olive oil
4 large shallots, sliced thin
8 large cloves garlic, minced
1 pound medium cremini mushrooms,
    halved lengthwise
¼ cup dry white wine
2 tablespoons shoyu or natural soy sauce
¼ cup minced fresh parsley or chervil

Set a wok over medium-high heat. Add the oil and tilt the pan to coat the sides. Add the shallots and garlic and stir-fry for 2 to 3 minutes. Add the mushrooms and continue stir-frying for 2 to 3 minutes. Add the wine and shoyu and cook, stirring, until the liquid is almost gone. Stir in the parsley or chervil and serve immediately.

Serves 4

Variations:
- Substitute 1 medium onion, chopped fine, for the shallots.
- Thinly slice 4 medium stalks asparagus on the diagonal and add them along with the mushrooms.

Calories: 110	Total fat: 4 g	Protein: 2 g
Carbohydrates: 10 g	Cholesterol: 0 g	Sodium: 527 mg

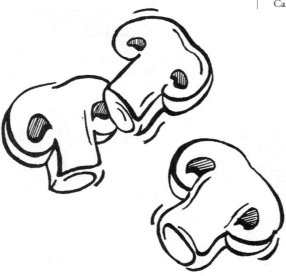

Colorful Caponata

When eggplants ripen and zucchini and tomatoes are taking over the garden and marketplace, make this spirited, versatile Italian relish. Serve it as an appetizer, salad, condiment, pita sandwich filling, or pasta topping. Celery is a traditional component; substitute it for the fennel if you prefer.

1 pound eggplant, peeled if desired and
    diced
Salt as needed
4 to 6 teaspoons extra-virgin olive oil
1 medium red onion, chopped fine
1 tablespoon minced garlic
1 medium red bell pepper, diced fine
½ cup finely chopped fennel bulb
1 small green or golden zucchini, diced fine
Freshly ground black pepper to taste
1 medium tomato, diced
1 tablespoon capers
⅓ cup chopped pitted kalamata olives
3 tablespoons red wine vinegar
1 tablespoon minced fresh basil leaves
1 teaspoon minced fresh lemon thyme **or**
    ½ teaspoon dried thyme

Place the eggplant dice in a colander and sprinkle generously with salt. Set aside for about an hour, then rinse and pat dry.

Set a wok over medium-high heat. Add 1 teaspoon oil and tilt the pan to coat the sides. Add the onion and stir-fry for about 1 minute. Continue to stir-fry, gradually adding the garlic, bell pepper, fennel, and zucchini, until the vegetables are just tender. Grind in some black pepper and transfer to a mixing bowl.

Wipe out the wok, then reheat. Pour 1 tablespoon oil around the rim and swirl it in the pan. Add the eggplant dice and stir-fry for several minutes, adding the remaining oil, if necessary, until the eggplant is tender. Combine with the stir-fried vegetables. Stir in the tomato, capers, olives, vinegar, basil, and thyme. Season with more black pepper and salt to taste. Serve hot, at room temperature, or chilled; the flavor improves as the ingredients mingle.

Makes about 4 cups

Per ½-cup serving
Calories: 76
Carbohydrates: 8 g
Total fat: 4 g
Cholesterol: 0 g
Protein: 0 g
Sodium: 156 mg

Anise–Flavored Eggplant

Eggplant takes well to braising. Ingredients and seasonings in this dish straddle Asian and Italian cuisines. Serve it with rice and something colorful, such as Green Beans and Carrots Sesame (page 30).

1 pound (about 4) Japanese eggplants
1 large onion
1 medium fennel bulb
1 tablespoon peanut oil
8 large cloves garlic, minced
Freshly ground black pepper to taste
1 cup vegetable stock
2 tablespoons tamari
Salt to taste
¼ cup minced fresh fennel leaves

Trim the ends off the eggplants and halve them lengthwise. Cut each half crosswise into thirds, then slice each piece lengthwise into thick strips. Cut the onion in half lengthwise, then cut each half into thin vertical slices. Cut the hard core out of the fennel, then cut it into thin vertical slices about 2 inches long.

Set a wok over high heat. Add the oil and swirl it to coat the sides of the pan. Add the onion and stir-fry for about 2 minutes, until translucent. Add the fennel and garlic, then gradually add the eggplant, continuing to stir-fry several minutes longer. Grind in the black pepper.

Add the stock and tamari and bring to a simmer. Cover the wok, reduce the heat, and simmer for 20 to 30 minutes, stirring occasionally, until the eggplant is thoroughly tender. Taste and add salt and more pepper if needed. Sprinkle in the fennel leaves just before serving.

Serves 4

Calories: 103	Total fat: 4 g	Protein: 2 g
Carbohydrates: 15 g	Cholesterol: 0 g	Sodium: 610 mg

Mexican Marinata

This colorful, crisp stir-fry brings to mind the piquant pickled vegetables often served at the most authentic Mexican restaurants.

1 tablespoon canola oil

1 medium onion, chopped

2 large cloves garlic, minced

1 jalapeño or other hot chile, seeded and minced, or to taste

1 medium carrot, halved lengthwise, then sliced on a diagonal

1 medium red bell pepper, sliced thin

½ cup peeled jícama or kohlrabi, cut into thin strips

2 cups small cauliflower florets

1 cup green beans, cut 1½ to 2 inches long on a diagonal

1 to 2 small green or golden zucchini, halved lengthwise, then sliced on a diagonal

Freshly ground black pepper to taste

½ teaspoon salt, plus more to taste

¼ to ½ cup vegetable stock as needed for steaming

1 tablespoon minced fresh marjoram, or 1½ teaspoons dried

1 tablespoon fresh lime juice

¼ cup toasted pumpkin seeds (optional; see note)

Set a wok over high heat. Pour the oil around the rim and swirl it in the pan to coat the sides. Add the onion and stir-fry for about 2 minutes, until translucent. Add the garlic, chile, and carrot and continue to stir-fry for several minutes, gradually adding the bell pepper, jícama, cauliflower, green beans, and zucchini. Grind in black pepper and add ½ teaspoon salt and ¼ cup stock.

Bring the stock to a simmer, cover the wok, and reduce the heat to medium. Steam for several minutes, adding more stock a tablespoon at a time if needed and stirring occasionally, until the vegetables are crisp-tender. Remove from the heat.

Stir in the marjoram and lime juice. Taste and add more salt as necessary. Garnish with the pumpkin seeds if desired.

Serves 4

Note: To toast pumpkin seeds, place them in a dry wok or heavy-bottomed skillet over low to medium heat. Roast the seeds for several minutes, stirring or shaking the pan often to prevent burning, until they begin popping and are lightly browned and toasty tasting.

Calories: 99   Total fat: 3 g   Protein: 2 g
Carbohydrates: 14 g   Cholesterol: 0 g   Sodium: 347 mg

One Potato, Two Potato

Try these for brunch, lunch, or dinner. They may become your favorite fried potatoes.

2 medium-large sweet potatoes or garnet
*   yams*
4 medium potatoes
3 to 4 teaspoons extra-virgin olive oil
2 to 3 teaspoons minced garlic
Freshly ground black pepper to taste
½ teaspoon freshly grated nutmeg
½ teaspoon salt or to taste

Peel the sweet and white potatoes and cut them into 2-inch-long, ½-inch-thick strips. Steam them separately, until tender but still firm.

Set a wok over medium heat. Pour the oil around the rim and tilt the pan to coat the sides. Add the garlic and stir-fry for about 30 seconds. Add the sweet potatoes and continue stir-frying for 2 to 3 minutes. Add the potatoes; cook, stirring often, for 15 to 20 minutes, until all the potatoes are slightly browned. Add the pepper, nutmeg, and salt; cook, stirring, for 2 to 3 minutes longer.

Serves 4

Calories: 269   Total fat: 4 g   Protein: 3 g
Carbohydrates: 56 g   Cholesterol: 0 g   Sodium: 284 mg

Simple Sweet and Sour Cabbage

Balsamic vinegar balances cabbage's naturally sweet flavor with just enough tartness. Serve this side dish hot or chilled.

2 teaspoons extra-virgin olive or canola oil
1 medium red or yellow onion, sliced thin
4 large cloves garlic, minced
4 cups thinly sliced red or green cabbage
2 tablespoons balsamic vinegar
Freshly ground black pepper to taste
Salt to taste

Set a wok over medium-high heat. Pour the oil around the rim and tilt the pan to coat the sides. Add the onion and stir-fry for 2 to 3 minutes, until translucent. Stir in the garlic. Gradually add the cabbage, continuing to stir-fry for several minutes, until the cabbage is cooked but still slightly crisp.

Remove the wok from the heat and add the vinegar, pepper, and salt; toss thoroughly.

Serves 4

Variation: Add 2 tablespoons dried currants along with the cabbage.

Calories: 59   Total fat: 2 g   Protein: 1 g
Carbohydrates: 8 g Cholesterol: 0 g   Sodium: 10 mg

Green Beans and Carrots Sesame

This simple vegetable dish is a flavorful, colorful addition to summer meals.

6 tablespoons vegetable stock or water
1 large carrot, halved lengthwise and sliced thin on a diagonal
½ pound green beans, sliced on a diagonal to match carrots
2 medium scallions, sliced on a diagonal
1 tablespoon shoyu or natural soy sauce
1 teaspoon dark sesame oil
1 tablespoon toasted sesame seeds

Add the stock to a wok and heat to boiling over high heat. Add the carrot and beans. Cover the wok and cook for 3 to 5 minutes, stirring occasionally, until the vegetables are just tender and the liquid has just about cooked away. Stir in the scallions and remove the wok from the heat.

Add the shoyu and oil to the vegetables and toss to coat them thoroughly. Add the sesame seeds and toss again.

Serves 4

Calories: 52	Total fat: 2 g	Protein: 1 g
Carbohydrates: 7 g	Cholesterol: 0 g	Sodium: 267 mg

Zucchini with Zip

Fresh mint and lemon add zest to this simple stir-fry; carrot contributes extra color.

1 tablespoon extra-virgin olive oil
1 large carrot, julienned
4 small green zucchini, julienned
2 scallions, sliced thin on a diagonal
Freshly ground black pepper to taste
2 teaspoons fresh lemon juice
2 tablespoons minced fresh mint
Salt to taste

Set a wok over medium-high heat. Pour the oil around the rim and swirl it to coat the sides. Add the carrot and stir-fry for 2 to 3 minutes. Add the zucchini and scallions and continue stir-frying for 1 to 2 minutes, until the carrot and zucchini are both crisp-tender. Grind in black pepper and stir-fry briefly.

Remove the wok from the heat and add the lemon juice, mint, and salt to taste. Serve immediately.

Serves 4

Variation: Omit the carrot and use twice as much zucchini: half green and half golden.

Calories: 44	Total fat: 2 g	Protein: 0 g
Carbohydrates: 3 g	Cholesterol: 0 g	Sodium: 7 mg

Rainbow Peppers and Red Onion

This is a great addition to a late-summer meal. Toss it with some pasta, and you have dinner.

1 tablespoon extra-virgin olive oil
1 medium to large red onion, halved
    lengthwise and sliced thin
2 large cloves garlic, minced
1 medium red bell pepper, sliced into thin
    2-inch-long strips
1 medium green bell pepper, sliced to match
    red pepper
1 medium yellow or orange bell pepper,
    sliced to match red pepper
Freshly ground black pepper to taste
1 tablespoon balsamic vinegar
1 tablespoon minced fresh basil
Salt to taste

Set a wok over medium-high heat. Pour the oil around the rim and swirl it to coat the sides. Add the onion and stir-fry for about 1 minute. Add the garlic, then gradually add the peppers. Continue to stir-fry for about 5 minutes longer, until the vegetables are tender. Grind in black pepper and add the vinegar and basil. Season with salt. Serve hot or at room temperature.

Serves 4

Calories: 71   Total fat: 2 g   Protein: 1 g
Carbohydrates: 8 g   Cholesterol: 0 g   Sodium: 4 mg

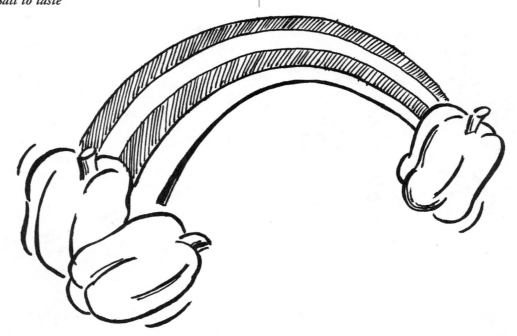

Summer Sisters Stir-Fry

The Iroquois called their major crops *the three sisters*: bean vines twined around sturdy corn stalks, and broad-leafed squash kept the earth under the corn from drying out. This simple, vividly colored stir-fry demonstrates that the three plants' flavors and textures are highly complementary, too.

1 tablespoon extra-virgin olive oil
1 large onion, chopped fine
3 large cloves garlic, minced
1 small to medium red bell pepper, diced fine
1 small to medium green bell pepper, diced fine
1½ cups green beans, cut into 1-inch lengths and lightly steamed
1½ cups fresh uncooked corn kernels
1½ cups diced zucchini or other summer squash
2 tablespoons minced fresh dill
Freshly ground black pepper to taste
Salt to taste

Set a wok over medium-high heat. Pour the oil around the rim and swirl it to coat the sides of the pan. Add the onion and stir-fry for 2 to 3 minutes, until it appears translucent. Stir in the garlic and continue stir-frying, gradually adding the bell peppers, beans, corn, and zucchini. When the vegetables are tender, add the dill, black pepper, and salt to taste.

Serves 4

| Calories: 135 | Total fat: 2 g | Protein: 3 g |
| Carbohydrates: 23 g | Cholesterol: 0 g | Sodium: 10 mg |

Spring Fling

This quickly prepared refreshing side dish features early spring vegetables. To make a light meal, serve it over udon or other noodles.

1½ teaspoons canola oil
½ to 1 cup thinly sliced ramps (wild
    scallions) or scallions, white and green
    parts kept separate
½ cup julienned carrot
½ teaspoon grated peeled fresh ginger
¼ pound asparagus, sliced ¼ inch thick on
    a diagonal, stalks and tips kept
    separate
¼ pound fresh oyster mushrooms,
    sliced if large
½ cup thinly sliced red radish
Freshly ground black pepper to taste
½ teaspoon salt, plus more to taste
2 tablespoons vegetable stock
1 tablespoon fresh lemon juice
4 cups small spinach leaves, well rinsed
2 teaspoons toasted sesame seeds

Set a wok over high heat. Add the oil and swirl it to coat the inside of the pan. Add the white portion of the ramps and stir-fry briefly. Add the carrot and ginger and continue stir-frying, gradually adding the asparagus stalks, mushrooms, radish, and asparagus tips. Add some black pepper, salt, and the stock, a tablespoon at a time.

When the vegetables are tender, add the lemon juice and green part of the ramps. Toss well, taste, and add more salt if needed. Serve on a bed of spinach, sprinkled with sesame seeds.

Serves 4

Calories: 62   Total fat: 2 g   Protein: 2 g
Carbohydrates: 7 g   Cholesterol: 0 g   Sodium: 318 mg

Brussels Sprouts with Pears and Hazelnuts

Take care not to overcook these mini-cabbages! Sweet pears, cider, and nutmeg wonderfully complement their naturally assertive cruciferous flavor. Substitute other pear varieties for the Bartletts, if you'd like.

1 pound small brussels sprouts
½ teaspoon salt, plus more to taste
½ cup water
1 teaspoon fresh lemon juice
2 medium Bartlett pears, peeled, cored, and diced
¼ cup apple cider
Pinch of freshly grated or ground nutmeg
¼ cup chopped toasted and skinned hazelnuts (see note)

Rinse the brussels sprouts. Cut off the stem ends and remove any discolored outer leaves.

Combine the sprouts, salt, and water in a wok over high heat. When the water comes to a boil, reduce the heat, cover the wok, and simmer for about 5 minutes, shaking the pan occasionally to rearrange the sprouts. When the sprouts are just easy to pierce to the center with a knife or sharp-pronged fork, remove the wok from the heat, drain the sprouts thoroughly, and transfer to a bowl. Toss with the lemon juice.

Add the pears, cider, and nutmeg to the wok. Bring to a gentle simmer and cook, stirring occasionally, for about 5 minutes or until the liquid is reduced considerably. Stir in the brussels sprouts and hazelnuts; heat briefly, stirring. Add more salt if needed and serve.

Serves 4

Note: Toast the hazelnuts for 10 minutes in a preheated 350ºF oven. Wrap the nuts in a towel and rub vigorously to remove their somewhat bitter-tasting skin—it may not all come off, but no matter.

Calories: 144	Total fat: 4 g	Protein: 3 g
Carbohydrates: 22 g	Cholesterol: 0 g	Sodium: 292 mg

Collards and Carrots

Look for tender young greens for this tasty, calcium-rich dish.

1 pound collard greens

1 to 2 tablespoons mellow barley or rice miso

2 tablespoons vegetable stock or more as needed

1 tablespoon lemon juice

1 tablespoon canola oil

1 large leek, white part only, halved lengthwise, sliced thin, and well rinsed

4 large cloves garlic, minced

1 large carrot, roll-cut (page 9) into thin 1-inch-long slices

With a sharp knife, slice the leafy part of the collards off the stalks and finely chop the leaves and stalks separately. An easy way to chop the leaves is to stack several together, roll them into a tight bundle, and slice through the roll. Then chop the long shreds into shorter pieces.

Whisk 1 tablespoon of the miso, 2 tablespoons of stock, and the lemon juice to a smooth paste.

Set a wok over high heat. Pour the oil around the rim, then tilt the pan to coat the sides. Add the leek and stir-fry for about 1 minute. Add the garlic, carrot, and sliced collard stalks and continue stir-frying for several minutes, until just tender. Gradually add the chopped collard leaves, stirring constantly, until they are wilted and tender but preferably still bright green. Stir in the miso mixture. Taste and add more diluted miso or salt if needed.

Serves 4

Note: Tougher collards may require a bit of steaming to tenderize. After stir-frying, add vegetable stock, a tablespoon or two at a time, cover the wok and steam, stirring occasionally, until the greens are tender.

Calories: 97	Total fat: 4 g	Protein: 2 g
Carbohydrates: 13 g	Cholesterol: 0 g	Sodium: 45 mg

Broccoli and Butternut Squash

Serve this classy, colorful side dish for a special holiday meal.

1 tablespoon walnut or light sesame oil
1 large leek, white part only, halved
  lengthwise, sliced thin, and well rinsed
2 cups diced peeled butternut squash
½ cup vegetable stock
2 tablespoons dry sherry
½ teaspoon salt, plus more to taste
4 cups broccoli, cut into small florets
  and stems
2 to 3 teaspoons minced fresh dill, **or**
  1 teaspoon dried
¼ cup chopped toasted walnuts
Freshly ground black pepper to taste

Set a wok over medium-high heat. Pour the oil around the rim and swirl it to coat the inside of the pan. Add the leek and stir-fry for about 1 minute. Add the squash and continue stir-frying for 2 to 3 minutes.

Add the stock, sherry, and ½ teaspoon salt. Bring the liquid to a simmer. Cover the wok, lower the heat, and steam about 5 minutes or until the squash is almost tender and the liquid is reduced considerably.

Add the broccoli and dill to the wok. Cover and steam for 2 to 3 minutes longer, until the broccoli is tender but still bright green. Add the walnuts. Season with pepper and more salt to taste. Serve immediately.

Serves 4

Calories: 175   Total fat: 8 g   Protein: 4 g
Carbohydrates: 20 g   Cholesterol: 0 g   Sodium: 339 mg

4

SAVORY STEWS

Stews are stir-fries with a bit of simmering tacked on to the end. A large wok or stir-fry pan is a special ally when cooking for a crowd. But whether you have company or not, stewing in quantity is entirely appropriate, because these dishes almost invariably taste best served as leftovers, after their flavors have had an opportunity to meld.

High-protein legumes are common to many of these medleys and make them complete meals when served with a simple grain or chewy bread and perhaps quick-cooked greens or a raw salad for some complementary crunch. Specific directions for cooking beans from scratch are included in the Cooking Notes appendix (page 149). Home-cooked dried legumes are most economical and, I think, delicious, but high-quality commercial ones are readily available, too. Look for those without preservatives and excess salt.

Stews usually connote cold weather, but many of these easily prepared entrees are just as appealing in warmer months, especially when their components are in their peak seasons. September Stew has a clear timetable; Spanish Vegetable Ragout, Southwestern Posole, West African Groundnut Stew, and Three-Bean Chili are all less obvious candidates for the same early-autumn calendar slot. Plan on Provençal Summer Stew and Grand Gumbo at the height of the heat; both are fabulous with freshly picked corn. Simmer others throughout the year when you're seeking the subtly married flavors that sometimes only a stew can provide.

Spanish Vegetable Ragout

This flavor mélange is truly delectable and will be even better the next day. Serve it with a crusty loaf or spoon it over polenta ringed with peppery arugula or mixed baby greens.

1 tablespoon extra-virgin olive oil
1 large sweet onion, chopped
1 large carrot, sliced
8 cloves garlic, minced
1 large green or red bell pepper, diced
2 cups green beans, cut 1½ inches long on a diagonal
2 cups diced potato
2 cups diced tender young zucchini
½ pound cremini or white button mushrooms, sliced thick
2 teaspoons sweet paprika
Freshly ground black pepper to taste
2 medium tomatoes, peeled (page 151) and diced
1 bay leaf
½ teaspoon salt, plus more to taste
1 cup vegetable stock
¼ cup dry sherry
¼ cup mellow barley miso
2 tablespoons minced fresh parsley
8 to 12 large pitted and chopped green olives

Set a wok over medium-high heat. Pour in the oil and tilt the pan to coat the sides. Add the onion and stir-fry for 2 to 3 minutes, until it appears translucent. Add the carrot and garlic and continue stir-frying, gradually adding the bell pepper, beans, potato, zucchini, and mushrooms. Add the paprika and black pepper; cook, stirring constantly, about a minute longer. Stir in the tomatoes, bay leaf, and salt. Stir-fry for a minute or two, until the tomato begins to release its juice.

Add the stock and sherry and bring the liquid just to a simmer. Cover the wok and reduce the heat to low. Simmer for about 20 minutes, stirring occasionally, until the vegetables are tender.

In a small bowl, whisk together the miso and several tablespoons of hot stock from the wok. Stir this mixture back into the stew. Taste and add more pepper and salt as necessary. Serve hot, garnished with the parsley and olives to taste.

Serves 4

Calories: 279	Total fat: 5 g	Protein: 5 g
Carbohydrates: 48 g	Cholesterol: 0 g	Sodium: 564 mg

September Stew

This brightly colored stew showcases many late-summer/early-autumn flavors and textures. Serve it with mixed greens dressed with a mustardy vinaigrette and some crusty, chewy bread.

2 teaspoons extra-virgin olive oil
1 medium onion, chopped
6 to 8 cloves garlic, minced
1 medium green or red bell pepper, diced
2 cups diced peeled butternut squash
1 cup diced potato
1 cup green or yellow wax beans, cut
    1½ inches long on a diagonal
1 cup fresh uncooked corn kernels
1 cup diced zucchini or other summer
    squash
Freshly ground black pepper to taste
1 large tomato, diced
½ teaspoon salt, plus more to taste
1 cup bean cooking liquid or vegetable
    stock
2 cups cooked kidney beans (page 150)
2 teaspoons slivered fresh sage leaves
¼ cup minced fresh parsley

Set a wok over medium-high heat. Pour in the oil and swirl it to coat the sides of the pan. Add the onion and stir-fry for 2 to 3 minutes, until it appears translucent. Add the garlic and bell pepper and continue stir-frying, gradually adding the butternut squash, potato, beans, corn, and zucchini. Grind in black pepper. Stir in the tomato, ½ teaspoon salt, and the stock.

Bring the liquid to a simmer. Cover the wok, reduce the heat, and cook gently for 15 to 20 minutes, stirring occasionally, until the vegetables are tender. Stir in the kidney beans and sage and heat for several minutes. Taste and add more pepper and salt if needed. Stir in half the parsley. Serve immediately, garnished with the remaining parsley.

Serves 4

Calories: 286	Total fat: 3 g	Protein: 10 g
Carbohydrates: 55 g	Cholesterol: 0 g	Sodium: 287 mg

Southwestern Posole

Dried corn kernels cooked in a mixture of wood ashes, lime, and water relinquish their tough outer layer, without which they're known as *hominy* or *posole*. The latter term also denotes a robust stew that includes these chewy, subtly sweet morsels. This particular posole is perfect for chasing off the chill of early autumn. Serve it over rice or with chunks of crusty bread.

2 teaspoons light sesame oil
1 large onion, chopped
4 to 6 large cloves garlic, minced
1 medium carrot, diced
1 medium turnip, diced
1 medium red bell pepper, diced
1 jalapeño or serrano chile, seeded and
*   minced, or to taste*
2 cups diced peeled butternut squash
1 teaspoon chili powder
1 teaspoon dried oregano, preferably
*   Mexican*
1½ cups bean cooking liquid or vegetable
*   stock*
½ teaspoon salt, plus more to taste
1½ cups cooked or canned drained hominy
*   (see note)*
2 cups cooked anasazi or pinto beans
*   (page 150)*
2 tablespoons dark red miso
2 tablespoons chopped fresh cilantro

Set a wok over medium-high heat. Add the oil and tilt the pan to coat the sides. Add the onion and stir-fry for 2 to 3 minutes, until it appears translucent. Continue to stir-fry, gradually adding the garlic, carrot, turnip, bell pepper, chile, and squash, over the next several minutes. Add the chili powder and oregano; stir-fry for about 1 minute longer.

Add the stock and salt. Bring the liquid to a simmer. Stir in the hominy and beans. Cover the wok, reduce the heat, and cook gently for about 15 minutes or until the vegetables are tender and the flavors blended.

In a small bowl, whisk the miso with several tablespoons of the stew stock. Stir this mixture into the stew. Taste and add more salt if needed. Garnish each serving with cilantro.

Serves 4

Note: Canned hominy is available in ethnic markets and some supermarkets, shelved near canned corn. Dried hominy is available in ethnic markets and some natural foods stores; cook it according to package directions.

Calories: 289	Total fat: 3 g	Protein: 10 g
Carbohydrates: 54 g	Cholesterol: 0 g	Sodium: 799 mg

Creamy Cauliflower and Carrot Curry

Ladle this luscious, subtly coconut-flavored chunky sauce over basmati rice or a short cut of pasta. To reduce the fat, use "lite" coconut milk.

1 teaspoon cumin seeds
½ teaspoon coriander seeds
½ teaspoon ground turmeric
¼ teaspoon ground cinnamon
¼ teaspoon ground cardamom
¼ teaspoon freshly grated nutmeg or
    ⅛ teaspoon ground
Pinch cayenne pepper or to taste
2 teaspoons peanut oil
½ teaspoon black mustard seeds
1 large onion, chopped
4 large cloves garlic, minced
1 large carrot, sliced thin
1 medium red bell pepper, diced
1 teaspoon grated peeled fresh ginger
3 cups small cauliflower florets
½ teaspoon salt or more to taste
¼ cup vegetable stock, plus more as needed
1 cup coconut milk
1 tablespoon mellow barley miso
4 cups well-rinsed coarsely chopped spinach
    leaves
2 teaspoons fresh lemon juice
2 tablespoons chopped fresh cilantro

Grind together the cumin, coriander, turmeric, cinnamon, cardamom, nutmeg, and cayenne in a spice grinder or mortar and pestle. Set aside.

Set a wok over high heat. Pour in the oil and swirl it to coat the inside. Add the mustard seeds and heat just until they begin to pop. Add the onion and stir-fry for 2 minutes. Stir in the garlic, carrot, bell pepper, ginger, cauliflower, and spice mixture and stir-fry briefly.

Add the salt and the stock. Cover and steam for several minutes, adding more stock as necessary, until the carrot and cauliflower are tender.

Uncover the pan and reduce the heat to low. Whisk together the coconut milk and miso; stir this mixture into the vegetables in the wok. Heat gently, but do not boil. Stir in the spinach and lemon juice and heat just until the spinach barely wilts and is still bright green. Taste and add more salt if needed. Serve immediately, garnished with the cilantro.

Serves 4 with rice or pasta

Variation: Diced peeled butternut squash, sweet potatoes, or garnet yams are good additions to this dish.

Calories: 211	Total fat: 13 g	Protein: 3 g
Carbohydrates: 17 g	Cholesterol: 0 g	Sodium: 316 mg

Provençal Summer Stew

This dish provides a perfectly palatable way to consume the garden's or market's best offerings from mid- to late summer. Serve it with crusty bread, pasta, corn risotto, or grilled polenta, along with some good olives.

1 tablespoon extra-virgin olive oil
1 large onion, chopped
6 to 8 large cloves garlic, minced
1 large green or red bell pepper, diced
1 pound (about 4) Japanese eggplant, diced
2 cups diced tender young green or golden
　　zucchini
1 large tomato, peeled (page 151) and
　　diced
Freshly ground black pepper to taste
½ teaspoon salt or more to taste
1 to 2 tablespoons minced fresh basil leaves
1 to 2 teaspoons minced fresh oregano or ½
　　teaspoon dried
1 to 2 teaspoons minced fresh lemon thyme
　　or ½ teaspoon dried thyme
¼ cup minced fresh parsley
2 tablespoons mellow barley miso or to taste

Set a wok over medium-high heat. Pour the oil around the rim, then swirl it to coat the inside of the pan. Add the onion and stir-fry for 2 to 3 minutes, until translucent. Continue to stir-fry, gradually adding the garlic, bell pepper, eggplant, and zucchini.

Stir in the tomato, grind in black pepper, and add ½ teaspoon salt. Cover the wok, reduce the heat, and simmer for 15 to 20 minutes or until the vegetables are tender. Stir in the basil, oregano, and thyme to taste, along with half the parsley.

Whisk the miso with several tablespoons of hot liquid from the stew, then add this mixture to the wok. Add more miso or salt if needed. Serve garnished with the remaining parsley.

Serves 4

Variation: Green or yellow wax beans and new potatoes are good additions to this stew.

Calories: 130　　Total fat: 2 g　　Protein: 2 g
Carbohydrates: 22 g　　Cholesterol: 0 g　　Sodium: 281 mg

Portuguese Green Stew

Kale and potatoes have always been signature Portuguese staples. White beans add extra substance, flavor, and their wonderfully creamy consistency to this hearty stew. Serve it in bowls with a crusty chewy bread or over pasta; I like to line the plates with torn arugula and scatter some briny black olives over the top.

¼ pound tender kale
1 tablespoon extra-virgin olive oil
1 large leek (white part only), halved
    lengthwise, sliced, and well rinsed
4 large cloves garlic, minced
1 large carrot, sliced thin
4 small potatoes, diced
2 cups vegetable stock or water
½ teaspoon salt, plus more to taste
2 tablespoons mellow barley miso
2 tablespoons red wine vinegar
2 cups cooked navy beans (page 150)
Freshly ground black pepper to taste
2 tablespoons minced fresh parsley

With a sharp knife, strip the leafy part of the kale off the stems. Finely chop the leaves and stems separately.

Set a wok over medium-high heat. Pour the oil around the rim and tilt the pan to coat the sides. Add the leek and stir-fry for about 1 minute. Add the garlic, carrot, and kale stems; continue stir-frying for 2 to 3 minutes longer.

Add the potatoes, stock, and ½ teaspoon salt. Bring the stock to a simmer. Cover the wok, reduce the heat, and simmer gently for 10 to 15 minutes, or until the carrots and potatoes are tender.

Transfer several tablespoons of the hot stock to a small bowl. Add the miso and vinegar; whisk to a smooth paste.

Add the beans and kale leaves to the wok. Grind in some pepper. Cook until the kale is wilted and tender but still bright green. Stir in the miso mixture and parsley. Taste and add more salt and pepper if needed.

Serves 4

Calories: 277	Total fat: 4 g	Protein: 9 g
Carbohydrates: 49 g	Cholesterol: 0 g	Sodium: 444 mg

Garlicky Garbanzos

Serving Mediterranean or Mexican? This spirited, satisfying bean dish will go beautifully with rice, couscous, or pasta.

1 tablespoon extra-virgin olive oil
1 large red onion, chopped
8 to 12 large cloves garlic, minced
½ teaspoon ground coriander
1½ teaspoons ground cumin
Freshly ground black pepper to taste
3 cups cooked garbanzo beans (page 150)
1 cup bean cooking liquid or vegetable
   stock
2 to 3 tablespoons mellow barley miso
4 teaspoons fresh lemon juice
Salt to taste
½ cup minced fresh parsley or cilantro

Set a wok over medium-high heat. Pour the oil around the rim and tilt the pan to coat the sides. Add the onion and stir-fry for 2 to 3 minutes. Add the garlic and stir-fry for about 1 minute longer. Add the coriander, cumin, and black pepper; stir-fry briefly. Stir in the garbanzos. Add ¾ cup of the cooking liquid and bring it to a simmer. Cover the wok, reduce the heat, and simmer gently, stirring occasionally, for about 15 minutes.

Whisk the remaining ¼ cup cooking liquid with 2 tablespoons of the miso and the lemon juice. Stir this mixture into the beans and simmer for several minutes over low heat. Taste and add more pepper and miso (mixed with some of the hot bean stock) or salt if needed. Garnish with the parsley just before serving.

Serves 4

Calories: 284	Total fat: 6 g	Protein: 10 g
Carbohydrates: 46 g	Cholesterol: 0 g	Sodium: 16 mg

Grand Gumbo

Okra thickens this New Orleans–style vegetable stew. Serve it with long-grain rice, crusty French bread, or corn bread.

1 tablespoon extra-virgin olive oil
1 large onion, chopped
8 cloves garlic, minced
2 large red bell peppers, diced
2 cups green or yellow wax beans, cut
  1½ inches long on a diagonal
1 cup diced green or golden zucchini or
  other summer squash
1 pound new potatoes, diced
Freshly ground black pepper to taste
1 teaspoon celery seeds
Pinch of cayenne pepper or to taste
2 large tomatoes, peeled (page 151) and
  diced
1 teaspoon salt, plus more to taste
½ pound okra, sliced thick
2 tablespoons dark red miso
¼ cup vegetable stock
2 teaspoons fresh lemon juice
1 teaspoon gumbo filé powder
  (see Glossary)

Set a wok over medium-high heat. Pour the oil around the rim and swirl it to coat the sides. Add the onion and stir-fry for 2 to 3 minutes, until it appears translucent. Add the garlic and bell peppers and continue stir-frying for several minutes, gradually adding the beans, zucchini, and potatoes. Grind in some black pepper and add the celery seeds and cayenne; stir-fry briefly. Add the tomatoes and 1 teaspoon salt; cover the wok, reduce the heat, and simmer for about 10 minutes, stirring often, until the vegetables are all tender.

Add the okra to the wok; cook briefly, until it is just tender.

Whisk the miso and stock to a smooth paste and stir it into the vegetable mixture along with the lemon juice and filé powder. Taste and add more salt if needed. Serve immediately.

Serves 4

Calories: 250   Total fat: 5 g   Protein: 6 g
Carbohydrates: 47 g   Cholesterol: 0 g   Sodium: 560 mg

Golden Squash and Split Pea Dal

Winter squash adds substance and a subtle sweetness to this Indian-style split pea classic.

1 cup dried yellow split peas, sorted
* and rinsed*
1 3-inch strip kombu (optional)
3 cups water
½ teaspoon cumin seeds
½ teaspoon coriander seeds
½ teaspoon ground turmeric
2 teaspoons light sesame oil
1 medium to large onion, chopped
4 cloves garlic, minced
1 teaspoon grated peeled fresh ginger
Cayenne pepper or minced fresh chile
* to taste*
2 cups diced peeled butternut squash
½ teaspoon salt, plus more to taste
½ to ¾ cup vegetable stock or water
Freshly ground black pepper to taste

Combine the split peas, kombu, and water in a medium saucepan. Bring to a boil and skim off any foam that forms on top of the peas. Lower the heat and simmer, covered loosely, for 45 to 50 minutes or until tender.

Toast the cumin and coriander seeds separately in a dry, heavy-bottomed skillet, then grind together with the turmeric in a spice grinder or mortar and pestle.

Set a wok over medium-high heat. Pour the oil around the rim, then swirl it to coat the inside of the pan. Add the onion and stir-fry for 2 or 3 minutes, until it appears translucent. Add the garlic, ginger, spice mixture, and cayenne and continue to stir-fry for about 1 minute more.

Add the squash, ½ teaspoon salt, and ½ cup of the stock. Cover the wok and steam for several minutes, stirring occasionally and adding more stock if necessary, until the squash is tender. Stir in the cooked peas and season with black pepper and more salt to taste.

Serves 4

Calories: 233   Total fat: 2 g   Protein: 10 g
Carbohydrates: 41 g   Cholesterol: 0 g   Sodium: 321 mg

Moroccan Lentil Tagine

A tagine is a stew; in this case, lentils with vegetables, spices, dried apricots, and walnuts. Serve over basmati rice.

1 cup dried lentils, preferably petite French green lentils, picked over, rinsed, and drained

1 3-inch strip kombu (optional)

2 to 3 cups water

⅓ cup unsulphured dried apricots

2 teaspoons extra-virgin olive oil

1 medium to large onion, chopped

4 large cloves garlic, minced

1½ cups sliced fennel bulb

Freshly ground black pepper to taste

Pinch of cayenne pepper or to taste

½ teaspoon ground cumin

½ teaspoon ground turmeric

¼ teaspoon ground cinnamon

¼ teaspoon ground coriander

¼ to ½ cup vegetable stock

2 teaspoons fresh lemon juice

1 to 2 tablespoons mellow barley miso or salt to taste

¼ cup finely chopped fresh parsley

⅓ cup lightly toasted walnuts, chopped coarse

Combine the lentils, kombu, and two cups of the water in a medium saucepan. Bring to a simmer, cover, then cook over very low heat for 45 minutes, or until the lentils are tender but retain their shape. Add more water as necessary. Set aside.

Pour water to cover over the apricots in a small saucepan. Bring just to a boil, cover, reduce the heat, and simmer gently for about 5 minutes. Remove from the heat and cool. Drain the apricots, reserving the liquid, and slice into strips.

Set a wok over medium-high heat. Pour the oil around the rim and tilt the pan to coat the sides. Add the onion and stir-fry for 2 to 3 minutes, until it appears translucent. Add the garlic and fennel and continue stir-frying for 2 to 3 minutes. Add the black pepper, cayenne, cumin, turmeric, cinnamon, and coriander; cook, stirring constantly, for a minute longer. Add the lentils, apricots, and reserved apricot cooking water plus vegetable stock to equal ½ cup. Cover and simmer gently for about 10 minutes, until the vegetables are tender.

Whisk the lemon juice, 1 tablespoon of the miso, and about 2 tablespoons of stock to a smooth paste. Stir this into the wok mixture along with half the parsley. Taste and add more miso (or salt) if needed. Serve the tagine garnished with the walnuts and remaining parsley.

Serves 4

Calories: 298	Total fat: 8 g	Protein: 12 g
Carbohydrates: 43 g	Cholesterol: 0 g	Sodium: 76 mg

Adzuki Beans and Root Vegetables

A wok or stir-fry pan makes a fine bean pot. Serve this pleasantly piquant dish with rice or another cooked grain.

2 teaspoons light sesame oil
1 medium onion, chopped fine
2 to 4 cloves garlic, pressed or minced
1 medium carrot, chopped fine
1 medium turnip, chopped fine
1 teaspoon grated peeled fresh ginger
1 cup plus 2 tablespoons bean cooking
    liquid or vegetable stock
3 cups cooked adzuki beans (page 150)
2 tablespoons dark red miso or to taste
2 tablespoons chopped fresh cilantro

Set a wok over medium-high heat. Pour the oil around the rim and tilt the pan to coat the sides. Add the onion and stir-fry for 2 to 3 minutes, until translucent. Gradually add the garlic, carrot, turnip, and ginger as you continue to stir-fry for about 3 minutes.

Add 1 cup of the cooking liquid and the beans. Bring to a simmer, then cover, reduce the heat, and cook for 10 to 15 minutes, until the vegetables are tender.

Whisk together the miso and remaining 2 tablespoons of stock; stir this smooth paste into the beans. Cook briefly—do not boil! Taste and add more miso (whisked with a little stock or water) if needed. Garnish with the cilantro.

Serves 4

Calories: 297   Total fat: 2 g   Protein: 13 g
Carbohydrates: 54 g   Cholesterol: 0 g   Sodium: 42 mg

Brazilian-Style Black Beans

This is a variation on *feijoada*, a traditional Brazilian black bean dish. Serve it over rice or a combination of bulgur and quinoa.

1 tablespoon extra-virgin olive oil
1 large onion, chopped
4 cloves garlic, minced
1 cup sliced fennel bulb
Freshly ground black pepper to taste
1 bay leaf
3 cups cooked black (turtle) beans
   (page 150)
⅔ to 1 cup bean cooking liquid or
   vegetable stock
1 large orange
2 tablespoons dark red miso or to taste
2 tablespoons minced fresh parsley
Green or red salsa to taste

Set a wok over medium-high heat. Pour the oil around the rim, then tilt the pan to coat the surface. Add the onion and stir-fry for 2 to 3 minutes, until it appears translucent. Add the garlic and fennel and continue stir-frying for about 3 minutes. Grind in the black pepper and stir-fry briefly.

Add the bay leaf, beans, and ⅔ cup cooking liquid and bring to a simmer. Cover the wok, reduce the heat, and simmer gently for 5 to 10 minutes, adding more stock as needed until the vegetables are tender.

Finely grate the orange zest and stir it into the wok mixture. Peel and section the orange, then squeeze the remaining fiber in your hand to release the juice, catching it in a cup or small bowl. Whisk in 2 tablespoons of miso to form a smooth paste; if there isn't enough juice, add stock. Stir the orange sections and miso paste into the beans. Taste and add more miso, mixed with a bit of stock, as needed. Serve the beans hot, garnished with the parsley and salsa.

Serves 4

Calories: 269	Total fat: 5 g	Protein: 12 g
Carbohydrates: 45 g	Cholesterol: 0 g	Sodium: 32 mg

Three-Bean Chili

Serve this filling favorite with long-grain rice or crusty corn or French bread. Diced avocado and a bit of coarsely grated cheese are good additional garnishes.

1 tablespoon extra-virgin olive oil
1 medium to large onion, chopped
4 large cloves garlic, minced
1 small hot chile, seeded and minced, or to taste
1 medium carrot, sliced
1 medium rib celery, sliced
1 medium green bell pepper, diced
2 teaspoons ground cumin
½ teaspoon ground coriander
1 teaspoon chili powder
1 large tomato, diced
½ teaspoon salt
1 cup cooked kidney beans (page 150)
1 cup cooked black (turtle) beans (page 150)
1 cup cooked anasazi or pinto beans (page 150)
¼ cup bean cooking liquid or vegetable stock
1 to 2 tablespoons dark miso
1 to 2 teaspoons fresh lemon juice
2 tablespoons chopped fresh cilantro

Set a wok over medium-high heat. Pour the oil around the rim and swirl it to coat the inside of the pan. Add the onion and stir-fry 2 to 3 minutes, until it appears translucent. Add the garlic and chile and continue stir-frying for several minutes, gradually adding the carrot, celery, and bell pepper. Add the cumin, coriander, and chili powder; stir-fry briefly.

Stir in the tomato and ½ teaspoon salt. Cover the wok and simmer gently, stirring occasionally for about 15 minutes or until the vegetables are tender. Stir in the beans and simmer for 10 minutes longer.

Whisk together the stock and miso to taste and stir it into the chili. Add lemon juice to taste. Garnish with the cilantro.

Serves 4

Calories: 269	Total fat: 5 g	Protein: 12 g
Carbohydrates: 45 g	Cholesterol: 0 g	Sodium: 269 mg

Philippine Beans and Greens

There are no doubt myriad versions of this classic mellow Philippine stew. Serve it with basmati or jasmine rice for a simple one-dish meal.

1 cup dried mung beans
1 quart water
1 2-inch strip kombu (optional)
1 tablespoon peanut oil
1 large onion, chopped
4 to 6 cloves garlic, minced
1 medium carrot, cut into thin slivers
2 teaspoons grated peeled fresh ginger
Pinch of cayenne pepper or to taste
½ cup coconut milk
2 tablespoons mellow barley miso
2 teaspoons fresh lime juice
2 cups well-rinsed coarsely chopped arugula
*   or spinach leaves*

Sort and rinse the beans. Combine them with the water and kombu in a heavy-bottomed, medium pot. Bring to a boil, cover, reduce the heat, and simmer for 45 minutes or until the beans are tender. Drain the beans, reserving ¾ cup of the stock.

Set a wok over high heat. Pour the oil around the rim, then tilt the pan to coat the sides. Add the onion and stir-fry for about 2 minutes, until it appears translucent. Add the garlic and carrot; continue to stir-fry for 3 to 4 minutes, until the carrot is almost tender. Stir in the ginger and cayenne and stir-fry briefly. Add the reserved stock and bring it to a simmer. Add the beans, cover the wok, and reduce the heat to low. Cook gently for about 10 minutes, stirring occasionally.

Whisk the coconut milk and miso to a smooth paste. Add this mixture and the lime juice to the beans. Stir in the greens and remove from the heat.

Serves 4

Calories: 256	Total fat: 9 g	Protein: 8 g
Carbohydrates: 33 g	Cholesterol: 0 g	Sodium: 37 mg

West African Groundnut Stew

Peanut butter adds a rich creaminess to this spicy vegetable mélange. Serve it over millet, rice, or couscous.

1 tablespoon peanut or light sesame oil
1 large onion, chopped
6 to 8 large cloves garlic, minced
1 teaspoon grated peeled fresh ginger
1 large carrot, sliced
1 large red bell pepper, sliced
2 generous cups peeled, diced sweet potato
    or garnet yam
1 heaping cup chopped green cabbage
½ teaspoon ground coriander
Cayenne pepper to taste
1 cup chopped tomato
1 teaspoon salt, plus more to taste
¼ cup chunky peanut butter
1 cup vegetable stock
2 teaspoons fresh lemon juice
2 to 4 tablespoons finely chopped scallion,
    chives, or cilantro
2 tablespoons grated fresh coconut

Set a wok over medium-high heat. Pour the oil around the rim and swirl it to coat the pan. Add the onion and stir-fry for 2 to 3 minutes, until it appears translucent. Add the garlic and ginger and continue stir-frying, gradually adding the carrot, bell pepper, sweet potatoes, and cabbage. Add the coriander and cayenne and stir-fry briefly. Stir in the tomatoes and 1 teaspoon salt.

Whisk the peanut butter with 6 tablespoons of the stock. Whisk in the lemon juice and set the mixture aside.

Add the remaining stock to the wok and bring it to a simmer. Cover the wok, reduce the heat, and simmer gently, stirring occasionally, for 10 to 15 minutes, until the vegetables are tender.

Stir in the peanut butter mixture. Taste and add more salt if needed. Serve garnished with the scallion and coconut.

Serves 4

Calories: 315   Total fat: 15 g   Protein: 7 g
Carbohydrates: 37 g   Cholesterol: 0 g   Sodium: 638 mg

Japanese Layered Stew

Large vegetable and tofu chunks simmered in a thickened broth make wonderfully warming cold-weather fare. Serve this stew over short-grain rice.

4 teaspoons kuzu powder

5 cups plus 4 teaspoons vegetable stock or
    water

1 4-inch strip kombu

8 large fresh shiitake mushrooms, stemmed
    and sliced thick

1 large leek, white part only, sliced and
    well rinsed

1 large carrot, halved lengthwise and sliced
    thick

2 cups diced daikon radish

1 large sweet potato, peeled and diced

1 pound firm tofu, cut into 1-inch dice

¼ cup shoyu or natural soy sauce

¼ cup mirin

2 tablespoons mellow barley miso or more
    to taste

4 cups well-rinsed coarsely chopped spinach
    leaves

4 scallions, sliced thin

Combine the kuzu and cold stock in a bowl and set it aside.

Place the kombu in a wok. Add 4¾ cups of the stock and heat to boiling. Reduce the heat and simmer for 10 to 15 minutes, until the kombu softens somewhat. Drain the kombu, reserving the stock, and cut it into small squares. Return the kombu pieces to the wok.

Arrange the shiitakes, leek, carrot, daikon, and sweet potato in layers over the kombu. Pour in the kombu stock and bring it to a simmer. Cover the wok and simmer gently for 10 to 15 minutes, until the vegetables are tender.

Arrange the tofu dice on top, cover, and simmer for about 5 minutes longer, until the tofu is heated thoroughly.

Whisk the shoyu, mirin, 2 tablespoons miso, and the remaining ¼ cup stock with the dissolved kuzu. Add this mixture to the wok along with the spinach. Simmer, stirring, until the broth thickens somewhat and the spinach wilts but is still bright green. Serve garnished with the scallions.

Serves 4

Calories: 289   Total fat: 6 g   Protein: 15 g
Carbohydrates: 40 g   Cholesterol: 0 g   Sodium: 1518 mg

5

TOFU, TEMPEH, AND SEITAN SPECIALTIES

Kitchen utensils aren't the only things we Westerners have borrowed from the Orient. Traditional Eastern foods are making their way west too, and three of them are featured in this chapter. Developed as meat substitutes centuries ago, tofu, tempeh, and seitan are rich in protein and can project meatlike qualities, emphasized by specific preparation techniques. As soy products, tofu and tempeh may offer some special health benefits: studies have shown that soy foods might lower cholesterol and possibly prevent certain cancers and osteoporosis.

Tofu, or bean curd, produced by curdling soy milk and subsequently pressing out a large proportion of the liquid whey to form solid cakes, is well established in the West. It is at its meatiest when frozen and then thawed. Prefrozen or not, it develops a crispy, crusty exterior when stir-fried in hot oil. Otherwise it has more of a cheeselike character and often stands in for dairy products. Diced firm tofu has a soft, melt-in-your-mouth quality when steamed or simmered gently. Blended with a bit of oil and fresh lemon juice, it takes on a sour cream consistency, ideal for dishes such as dairyless Mushroom Stroganoff. Mashed tofu added to stir-fried vegetables makes an appetizing eggless scramble.

Tempeh and seitan are both naturally more meatlike than tofu. An ancient Indonesian soy product, tempeh is made by incubating cultured cooked cracked soybeans just long enough to bind them together with beneficial white mold. The end result is a flat, compact, tender yet chewy cake with a tantalizing yeasty aroma and mild, slightly mushroomy or nutty taste. Grains, nuts, or seeds are sometimes mixed with the soybeans to subtly vary a particular batch's flavor and texture. Use tempeh much like beef, pork, or poultry strips in meatless makeovers like Tempeh Teriyaki. Crumbled tempeh resembles ground beef.

Seitan, also called wheat meat, is most meaty of all. It begins with a stiff all-wheat bread dough that's kneaded under water to wash away the starch, leaving only the elastic, high-protein gluten. Freshly made seitan has an especially chewy texture. Commercially packaged preseasoned seitan is readily available in natural foods stores, food co-ops, and even some supermarkets. The recipes here feature traditionally seasoned seitan with a soy, ginger, and garlic flavor. *If you use unflavored seitan, add more garlic, plus ginger and shoyu or tamari to taste, and substitute vegetable stock for the commercial marinade if it's included in the recipe.* Seitan chunks hold their shape in stews, and strips satisfactorily simulate skirt steak in stir-fries.

All three of these centuries-old Asian products taste rather bland on their own but readily soak up marinades and seasonings of all kinds. As you'll see in the following recipes, they present myriad possibilities for dishes with diverse flavors and formats.

Tofu and Green Tomato Stir-Fry

Try this end-of-summer treat over corn pasta.

1 tablespoon extra-virgin olive oil
1 large onion, chopped
8 large cloves garlic, minced
1 jalapeño chile, seeded and minced, or to taste
1 large red bell pepper, diced fine
2 large green tomatoes, diced fine
1 teaspoon salt, plus more to taste
½ pound firm tofu, diced fine
Freshly ground black pepper to taste
¼ cup chopped fresh cilantro

Set a wok over medium-high heat. Add the oil and swirl it to coat the inside of the pan. Add the onion and stir-fry for 2 to 3 minutes, until translucent. Add the garlic, chile, and bell pepper and continue stir-frying for about 3 minutes. Stir in the tomatoes and 1 teaspoon salt. Cook for several minutes, stirring, until the vegetables are tender.

Stir in the tofu and continue cooking, stirring gently, until it is softened and heated through and the flavors are blended. Season with black pepper and more salt to taste. Stir in the cilantro and serve immediately.

Serves 4

Calories: 135   Total fat: 6 g   Protein: 5 g
Carbohydrates: 14 g   Cholesterol: 0 g   Sodium: 1046 mg

Scrambled Tofu

Try this no-cholesterol, faux-egg dish for breakfast with toast or roll it up in tortillas.

2 teaspoons canola or peanut oil
1 medium to large onion, chopped fine
4 cloves garlic, minced
1 medium to large red bell pepper,
    chopped fine
½ cup grated carrot
¾ teaspoon ground turmeric
1½ teaspoons ground cumin
Pinch of cayenne pepper or to taste
Freshly ground black pepper to taste
1½ pounds firm tofu, mashed
1½ teaspoons fresh lemon juice
1 teaspoon salt or to taste
⅓ cup chopped fresh cilantro

Set a wok over high heat. Pour in the oil and tilt the pan to coat the sides. Add the onion and stir-fry for about 2 minutes, until it appears translucent. Add the garlic, bell pepper, and carrot; continue to stir-fry for 1 to 2 minutes, until the vegetables are just tender.

Stir in the turmeric, cumin, cayenne, and black pepper; stir-fry briefly—less than a minute. Add the tofu and cook, stirring, for several minutes, until it's thoroughly combined with the other ingredients. Add the lemon juice and salt and remove from the heat. Sprinkle with cilantro and serve immediately.

Serves 4

Calories: 178	Total fat: 9 g	Protein: 12 g
Carbohydrates: 10 g	Cholesterol: 0 g	Sodium: 553 mg

Tofu Scallopine

Scaloppine means "thin slices," and they are typically made with tender veal. This recipe is named for the white wine, lemon, and herb sauce that usually goes with the meat. Serve it over pasta or long-grain rice.

4 teaspoons extra-virgin olive oil
1 large onion, chopped
4 large cloves garlic, minced
1 pound cremini or white button
    mushrooms, sliced thick
1 pound firm tofu, cut into ½-inch dice
2 teaspoons minced fresh thyme **or**
    1 teaspoon dried
½ cup dry white wine
¼ cup fresh lemon juice
4 cups well-rinsed coarsely chopped
    spinach leaves
2 tablespoons minced fresh parsley
Salt to taste
Freshly ground black pepper to taste
Thinly sliced red bell pepper (optional)

Set a wok over medium-high heat. Pour the oil around the rim, then tilt the pan to coat the sides. Add the onion and stir-fry for 2 to 3 minutes, until it appears translucent. Add the garlic and mushrooms; continue to stir-fry for about 3 minutes, until the mushrooms appear moist. Stir in the tofu and thyme; stir-fry for 2 to 3 minutes longer, taking care not to break up the tofu.

Add the wine and lemon juice. Bring to a simmer and cook, stirring often, for 3 to 4 minutes, until the liquid is reduced by about half. Add the spinach and parsley. Cook briefly, stirring, until the spinach wilts but is still bright green. Season with salt and pepper and serve immediately, garnished with the red bell pepper if desired.

Serves 4

Calories: 236	Total fat: 8 g	Protein: 11 g
Carbohydrates: 17 g	Cholesterol: 0 g	Sodium: 43 mg

Tofu à L'Orange

Who says tofu has to be bland and boring? This lively concoction will win over even strident naysayers. Serve it over regular long-grain or basmati rice or a combination of one or the other with wild rice.

2 teaspoons kuzu powder
4 teaspoons cold vegetable stock
1 to 2 tablespoons canola oil
1 pound firm tofu, well-pressed (page 151)
*   and cut into ½-inch dice*
1 large onion, chopped
8 cloves garlic, minced
2 teaspoons minced fresh thyme or
*   1 teaspoon dried*
Freshly ground black pepper to taste
1⅓ cups vegetable stock
⅔ cup fresh orange juice
¼ teaspoon finely grated orange zest
1 teaspoon salt plus more to taste
2 teaspoons fresh lemon juice
1 tablespoon white wine vinegar
¼ cup minced fresh parsley

Combine the kuzu and cold stock in a small bowl and set aside until the kuzu is dissolved thoroughly, about 2 minutes.

Set the wok over high heat. Add 1 tablespoon oil and the tofu. Stir-fry for several minutes, adding another teaspoon of oil if necessary, until the tofu is lightly browned on all sides. Remove the tofu from the wok.

Add the remaining oil to the wok, tilting the pan to coat the bottom and sides. Add the onion and stir-fry for 2 to 3 minutes, until it appears translucent. Add the garlic and stir-fry for a minute or two longer, until the onion is tender. Add the thyme and grind in some black pepper.

Add the vegetable stock and orange juice and bring to a simmer. Stir in the orange zest, 1 teaspoon salt, lemon juice, and vinegar. Simmer for several minutes, stirring occasionally, until the liquid reduces somewhat and the flavors meld. Stir in the tofu.

Reduce the heat and slowly add the dissolved kuzu, stirring constantly. Simmer gently until the sauce thickens. Add half the parsley. Taste and season with more salt and pepper if needed. Serve garnished with the remaining parsley.

Serves 4

Calories: 197	Total fat: 9 g	Protein: 9 g
Carbohydrates: 16 g	Cholesterol: 0 g	Sodium: 645 mg

Mushroom Stroganoff

Lighter and with less fat than the traditional dish, this version is still rich and creamy tasting. Serve it over noodles or kasha. Shiitake mushrooms add an interesting twist. Think ahead to soak them—or substitute stemmed fresh shiitakes and use vegetable stock in place of the soaking liquid.

1 ounce dried shiitake mushrooms
½ pound medium-firm tofu
½ teaspoon salt
2 tablespoons fresh lemon juice
4 teaspoons tahini
4 teaspoons canola oil
1 large onion, chopped fine
1 pound fresh cremini or white button
mushrooms, sliced thick
Freshly ground black pepper to taste
½ teaspoon sweet paprika, plus more
to taste
⅓ cup dry red wine
2 tablespoons shoyu or natural soy sauce, or
to taste
2 tablespoons minced fresh dill, plus more
to taste, or 1 tablespoon dried
1 teaspoon minced fresh thyme, or
½ teaspoon dried
¼ cup minced fresh parsley

Pour about 2 cups boiling water over the shiitakes in a bowl, cover, and set aside to soak for at least 30 minutes. Squeeze the liquid out of the mushrooms, cut off and discard their tough stems, and thinly slice the caps. Reserve the soaking liquid.

Combine the tofu, salt, lemon juice, and tahini in a food processor or blender and blend until thoroughly smooth; set aside.

Set a wok over high heat and pour the oil around the rim; tilt the pan to coat the sides. Add the onion and stir-fry for about 2 minutes, until it appears translucent. Add the sliced shiitakes and fresh mushrooms, some pepper, and ½ teaspoon paprika; continue to stir-fry for 2 to 3 minutes, until the fresh mushrooms no longer appear dry.

Add ¾ cup of the reserved mushroom-soaking liquid, the wine, and the shoyu. Cover and reduce the heat to medium-low; cook for several minutes, until the mushrooms are tender and the flavors melded. Stir in the dill and thyme, and the tofu mixture; cook briefly until thickened slightly. Serve immediately, garnished with the parsley and additional paprika if desired.

Serves 4

Calories: 232   Total fat: 9 g   Protein: 9 g
Carbohydrates: 20 g   Cholesterol: 0 g   Sodium: 802 mg

Fall Flavors Tofu

Serve this colorful, supremely satisfying stir-fry over millet, rice, or a combination of the two grains.

1 teaspoon dark sesame oil

2 tablespoons shoyu or natural soy sauce

½ pound tofu, well pressed (page 151) and
    cut into ½-inch dice

1 teaspoon kuzu powder

2 teaspoons cold vegetable stock

1 tablespoon light sesame or peanut oil

1 large onion, chopped

6 to 8 large cloves garlic, minced

2 teaspoons grated peeled fresh ginger

1 cup thickly sliced carrot

1 cup thickly sliced parsnip

2 cups sliced peeled sweet potato or
    garnet yam

8 2-inch-diameter fresh shiitake
    mushrooms, stemmed and sliced thin

2 cups vegetable stock

1 tablespoon fresh lemon juice

2 tablespoons mellow barley miso

4 cups well-rinsed coarsely chopped
    spinach leaves

Freshly ground black pepper to taste

Salt to taste

Mix together the dark sesame oil and shoyu in a shallow bowl. Add the diced tofu and stir gently to coat. Set it aside and stir occasionally.

Combine the kuzu and cold stock in a bowl. Set aside until the kuzu is dissolved thoroughly, about 2 minutes.

Set a wok over medium-high heat. Pour the light sesame oil around the rim and tilt the pan to coat the inside. Add the onion and stir-fry for 2 to 3 minutes, until translucent. Add the garlic, ginger, and carrot and continue stir-frying for several minutes, gradually adding the parsnip, sweet potato, and mushrooms. Pour in all but 2 tablespoons of the stock and bring it to a simmer. Cover the wok, reduce the heat, and simmer gently for 5 to 10 minutes, until the vegetables are tender. Add the tofu and steam briefly.

Add the fresh lemon juice, miso, and remaining 2 tablespoons stock to the dissolved kuzu. Whisk to a smooth paste. Add to the wok along with the spinach and some black pepper. Cook, stirring, until the liquid thickens. Taste and season with more pepper and salt if needed. Serve immediately.

Serves 4

Calories: 294	Total fat: 7 g	Protein: 8 g
Carbohydrates: 47 g	Cholesterol: 0 g	Sodium: 727 mg

Tofu Migas

Tofu stands in for eggs in this Tex-Mex specialty, and achiote turns it a bright yellow-orange. Serve it with warm soft corn or flour tortillas and a zesty fruit salsa.

1 teaspoon achiote
1 tablespoon light sesame or extra-virgin olive oil
1 large onion, chopped fine
4 large cloves garlic, minced
1 jalapeño chile, seeded and minced, or to taste
1 large green bell pepper, diced fine
2 teaspoons ground cumin
½ teaspoon ground coriander
2 medium tomatoes, diced
1 pound medium-firm tofu, crumbled into small pieces
1 teaspoon salt or to taste
4 corn tortillas, cut into ½- by 1½-inch strips
1 tablespoon fresh lime juice
¼ cup chopped fresh cilantro

Set a wok over medium-low heat. Add the achiote and oil and stir until the oil turns a bright reddish orange. Remove the seeds from the oil and discard.

Raise the heat to medium-high. Add the onion and stir-fry for 2 to 3 minutes, until translucent. Add the garlic, chile, and bell pepper and stir-fry 2 to 3 minutes longer. Add the cumin and coriander and stir-fry briefly. Stir in the tomatoes and continue stir-frying until the vegetables are tender.

Add the tofu and 1 teaspoon salt. Stir-fry until the tofu softens and the ingredients are well mixed. Add the tortilla strips and continue stir-frying a minute or two longer or until they soften. Stir in the lime juice and add more salt if needed. Add the cilantro and serve immediately.

Serves 4

| Calories: 238 | Total fat: 9 g | Protein: 11 g |
| Carbohydrates: 26 g | Cholesterol: 0 g | Sodium: 1048 mg |

Tofu and Broccoli Stir-Fry

Freezing gives tofu a light, spongy texture and makes it super-absorbent. Lots of lemon juice and fresh ginger add zing to this dish. Try it over noodles or rice.

1 pound firm tofu, frozen, thawed, and
*   well pressed (page 151)*
¼ cup plus 2 tablespoons shoyu or natural
*   soy sauce*
2 teaspoons dark sesame oil
¼ cup fresh lemon juice
1½ teaspoons kuzu powder
1 tablespoon cold vegetable stock or water
1 tablespoon peanut oil
1 large onion, sliced thin
8 cloves garlic, minced
4 teaspoons grated peeled fresh ginger
6 to 8 cups broccoli, cut into small florets
*   and stems*
¾ to 1 cup vegetable stock
2 to 4 teaspoons lightly toasted sesame seeds

Cut the tofu into ½-inch dice. In a bowl, whisk ¼ cup of the shoyu with the dark sesame oil and lemon juice. Add the tofu and marinate for 10 minutes or so, occasionally stirring gently.

Combine the kuzu and cold stock or water; set aside for 2 to 3 minutes, until the kuzu is dissolved thoroughly. Whisk in the remaining shoyu.

Set a wok over high heat. Pour the peanut oil around the rim, then tilt the pan to coat the sides. Add the onion and stir-fry for 2 to 3 minutes, until translucent. Stir in the garlic and ginger. Continue to stir-fry, gradually adding the broccoli.

Add the tofu, marinade, and ¾ cup of the stock. Cover the wok and steam briefly, until the broccoli is crisp-tender and still bright green. If necessary, add 2 to 4 tablespoons more stock and steam for 1 to 2 minutes longer.

Add the dissolved kuzu and shoyu mixture and stir constantly until the liquid thickens. Serve immediately, garnished with sesame seeds.

Serves 4

| Calories: 253 | Total fat: 12 g | Protein: 13 g |
| Carbohydrates: 22 g | Cholesterol: 0 g | Sodium: 1676 mg |

Thai Tempeh

For a festive dinner, serve this simple yet rich coconut-laced concoction with jasmine rice and a generous variety of vegetable dishes—the servings are small.

2 teaspoons peanut oil
1 8-ounce package tempeh
½ cup vegetable stock
1 teaspoon tamari
2 large cloves garlic, minced
1 small fresh red or green chile, minced,
    or cayenne pepper to taste
1 teaspoon grated peeled fresh ginger
½ cup coconut milk
2 large scallions, sliced thin
½ teaspoon salt or to taste
1 teaspoon fresh lime juice
2 to 4 tablespoons chopped fresh cilantro

Set a wok over medium-high heat. Pour in the oil and tilt the pan to coat the bottom. Add the tempeh and immediately flip it to coat both sides with oil. Brown the tempeh on both sides. Remove the tempeh and cut it into short thin strips.

Add the stock, tamari, garlic, chile, and ginger to the wok and bring to a simmer. Add the tempeh strips, cover the pan, and cook for several minutes, stirring occasionally, until the liquid has been absorbed.

Stir in the coconut milk, scallions, and ½ teaspoon salt. Simmer gently for several minutes over low heat.

Add the lime juice, and cilantro to taste. Taste and add more salt if needed. Serve immediately.

Serves 4 modestly

Variation: Add 1 medium carrot, sliced thin, along with the stock, tempeh strips, etc. Then add about 2 cups sliced spinach leaves along with the lime juice and cilantro and cook until just wilted but still bright green.

Calories: 199   Total fat: 11 g   Protein: 10 g
Carbohydrates: 12 g   Cholesterol: 0 g   Sodium: 395 mg

Tempeh Moutarde

*S*poon this sprightly sauced stir-fry over a rice and kasha or long-grain and wild rice combo on a bed of pungent arugula. Serve sauerkraut on the side.

2 teaspoons kuzu powder
1 tablespoon cold vegetable stock or water
2 tablespoons mellow barley miso
2 tablespoons prepared stone-ground
*   mustard*
2 teaspoons fresh lemon juice
2 cups vegetable stock
4 teaspoons canola oil
1 8-ounce package tempeh
1 large onion, chopped
4 large cloves garlic, minced
1 large carrot, roll-cut (page 9) into thin
*   1-inch-long slices*
1 large turnip, cut into thin 1-inch strips
3 cups cauliflower, cut into small
*   florets and stems*
3 cups broccoli, cut into small florets
Freshly ground black pepper to taste
2 teaspoons minced fresh dill **or**
*   1 teaspoon dried*

Combine the kuzu and cold stock in a small bowl and set it aside until dissolved, about 2 minutes. Add the miso, mustard, lemon juice, and ¼ cup of the stock; whisk until smooth.

Set a wok over medium heat. Add 2 teaspoons of the oil and the tempeh. Immediately turn the tempeh over to coat the second side with oil. Brown it on both sides. Remove the tempeh from the wok and slice it into pieces about 1 inch long and ¼ to ½ inch thick.

Set the wok over high heat. Add the remaining oil and tilt the pan to coat the sides. Add the onion and stir-fry for 2 to 3 minutes, until translucent. Add the garlic and carrot and continue stir-frying for about 5 minutes, gradually adding the turnip and cauliflower.

Add the tempeh and remaining stock. Bring the liquid to a simmer, cover the wok and steam for several minutes, until the vegetables are tender. Add the broccoli and steam for about 1 minute longer. Add black pepper, dill, and the kuzu mixture; cook, stirring, until the sauce thickens. Serve immediately.

Serves 4

Calories: 273	Total fat: 10 g	Protein: 13 g
Carbohydrates: 31 g	Cholesterol: 0 g	Sodium: 420 mg

Curried Tempeh

This vibrant tempeh and vegetable mixture over long-grain rice makes a meal.

2 teaspoons cumin seeds
1 teaspoon coriander seeds
1 teaspoon ground turmeric
2 teaspoons plus 1 tablespoon peanut oil
1 8-ounce package tempeh
1 large onion, chopped
6 cloves garlic, minced
1 jalapeño or other small hot chile, seeded
   and minced, or to taste
1 large carrot, halved lengthwise and sliced
   on a diagonal
1 large green bell pepper, diced
3 cups cauliflower, cut into small
   florets and stems
2 small to medium potatoes, diced
4 plum tomatoes, peeled (page 151) and
   diced
1 teaspoon grated peeled fresh ginger
1 tablespoon minced fresh lemongrass
½ teaspoon salt, plus more to taste
1 cup vegetable stock
1 tablespoon fresh lime juice
2 to 4 tablespoons chopped fresh cilantro

Toast the cumin and coriander seeds separately in a dry heavy-bottomed skillet; cool somewhat. Grind together with the turmeric, using a spice grinder or mortar and pestle.

Set a wok over medium heat. Add 2 teaspoons of the oil and the tempeh. Immediately turn the tempeh to coat both sides with oil, then brown it on both sides. Remove the tempeh from the wok, cool, and cut it into short strips or dice.

Add the remaining tablespoon oil to the wok over medium-high heat and swirl it to coat the inside of the pan. Add the onion and stir-fry about 3 minutes, or until translucent. Add the garlic and chile and continue stir-frying, gradually adding the carrot, green pepper, cauliflower, and potatoes. Add the spice mixture and stir-fry briefly, taking care not to burn the spices.

Stir in the tomatoes, ginger, lemongrass, tempeh, and ½ teaspoon salt. Stir-fry for 2 to 3 minutes longer, then add the stock and bring it to a simmer. Cover the wok, reduce the heat, and cook, stirring occasionally, for about 10 minutes or until the vegetables are tender and the liquid is reduced.

Add the lime juice and more salt to taste. Serve garnished with the cilantro to taste.

Serves 4

Calories: 300   Total fat: 9 g   Protein: 12 g
Carbohydrates: 39 g   Cholesterol: 0 g   Sodium: 407 mg

Tijuana Tempeh

Here's a stir-fry with Mexican tastes. The tempeh absorbs a soy-lime flavor as it simmers. Basmati or Texmati rice is a perfect accompaniment.

¾ cup vegetable stock
2 tablespoons shoyu or natural soy sauce
¼ cup fresh lime juice
4 teaspoons light sesame oil
1 8-ounce package tempeh
2 medium-sized red or yellow onions,
    sliced thin
6 to 8 large cloves garlic, minced
1 jalapeño or serrano chile, seeded and
    minced, or to taste
2 medium red bell peppers, cut into
    1½-inch strips
4 small zucchini, cut into 1½-inch strips
¼ cup chopped fresh cilantro
1 ripe avocado, peeled, pitted, and diced
    (optional)

Whisk together the stock, shoyu, and lime juice.

Set a wok over medium heat. Add 2 teaspoons of the oil and the tempeh, turning it to coat both sides. Brown the tempeh on both sides. Remove it from the wok and cut it into strips about ½ inch thick and 1½ inches long; set aside.

Reheat the wok over medium-high heat and add the remaining 2 teaspoons oil, swirling it to coat the sides of the pan. Add the onions and stir-fry for 2 to 3 minutes, until translucent. Add the garlic, chile, and red bell peppers and continue stir-frying for 2 minutes more. Add the zucchini and tempeh and stir-fry about 1 minute. Add the liquid seasoning mixture. Cover the wok and cook for several minutes, stirring often, until the vegetables are tender and the liquid is almost absorbed. Serve immediately, garnished with the cilantro, and avocado if desired.

Serves 4

Calories: 216	Total fat: 8 g	Protein: 11 g
Carbohydrates: 23 g	Cholesterol: 0 g	Sodium: 580 mg

Tempeh, Beet, and Carrot Stir-Fry

Tempeh contributes a "meaty" substance to this hearty main dish. Pungent fresh ginger is a terrific foil for the sweet root vegetables. I especially like to serve this gorgeous rich red stir-fry over kasha or wild rice tossed with basmati rice. Cooked greens and sauerkraut are tasty accompaniments.

2 teaspoons kuzu powder
4 teaspoons cold stock or water
4 teaspoons fresh lemon juice
2 tablespoons mellow barley miso
2 cups vegetable stock or beet cooking
 liquid
4 teaspoons light sesame or canola oil
1 8-ounce package tempeh
1 large onion, sliced lengthwise into thin
 crescents
2 medium carrots, roll-cut (page 9) into
 thin, 1½-inch-long slices
4 medium beets, cooked, peeled, and cut
 into thin, 1½-inch-long strips
1 tablespoon grated peeled fresh ginger
Freshly ground black pepper to taste
2 tablespoons minced fresh dill or
 1 tablespoon dried
Salt to taste

Combine the kuzu and cold stock in a small bowl and set aside until dissolved, about 2 minutes. Add the lemon juice, miso, and ¼ cup of the stock; whisk until thoroughly smooth.

Set a wok over medium-high heat. Add 2 teaspoons of the oil and then the tempeh, turning it immediately to coat both sides with oil. Brown the tempeh on both sides. Remove from the pan and slice it into strips ¼ to ½ inch thick and 1½ inches long.

Add the remaining 2 teaspoons oil to the wok. Add the onion and stir-fry for 2 to 3 minutes, until translucent. Add the carrots and continue stir-frying for several minutes. Stir in the beets, ginger, pepper, remaining 1¾ cups stock, and tempeh strips. Cover the wok, reduce the heat, and simmer for several minutes, until the vegetables are tender.

Add the kuzu mixture to the wok and stir gently until the sauce thickens. Stir in half the dill. Season with salt. Serve immediately, garnished with the remaining dill.

Serves 4

Calories: 229   Total fat: 8 g   Protein: 11 g
Carbohydrates: 26 g   Cholesterol: 0 g   Sodium: 47 mg

Tempeh Mushroom Marsala

Serve this hearty mushroom and tempeh mixture over long-grain rice, wild rice, or kasha.

1 cup boiling water
½ ounce dried porcini mushrooms
1 pound combined fresh cremini,
    portobello, and shiitake mushrooms
½ cup marsala (see Glossary)
2 tablespoons mellow barley miso
4 teaspoons extra-virgin olive oil
1 8-ounce package tempeh
1 large onion, chopped
8 large cloves garlic, minced
2 teaspoons minced fresh thyme or
    1 teaspoon dried
Freshly ground black pepper to taste
¼ cup minced fresh parsley
Salt to taste

Pour the boiling water over the porcini and set them aside to soak for about 30 minutes. Drain well, reserving the soaking water. Thinly slice the mushrooms.

Separate the fresh mushroom caps and stems. Save the shiitake stems for making stock; slice the caps. Slice the cremini and portobello stems and caps separately.

Whisk together the marsala and miso; set aside.

Add 2 teaspoons of the oil to a wok over medium heat. Add the tempeh and turn immediately to coat both sides with oil. Brown it well, then remove from the wok and cut into strips about 1 inch long and ½ inch wide.

Pour the remaining 2 teaspoons oil into the wok over medium-high heat and swirl it to coat the bottom and sides. Add the onion and stir-fry for 2 to 3 minutes or until translucent. Stir in the garlic, mushroom stems, thyme, and black pepper. Continue to stir-fry, gradually adding the sliced porcini and fresh mushroom caps, and cook until the mushroom caps appear moist. Stir in the tempeh and marsala-miso mixture, reduce the heat, and cook gently for several minutes. Remove from the heat and add the parsley. Season with salt. Serve immediately.

Serves 4

Calories: 249	Total fat: 8 g	Protein: 12 g
Carbohydrates: 28 g	Cholesterol: 0 g	Sodium: 16 mg

Tempeh Teriyaki

Tempeh soaks up a sweet and sour marinade, then teams up with a colorful combination of vegetables in this satisfying cool-season stir-fry. Serve it over long-grain rice.

¼ cup tamari
2 teaspoons Sucanat or light brown sugar
2 tablespoons dry sherry
1¼ cups vegetable stock or water
1 8-ounce package tempeh
2 teaspoons kuzu powder
4 teaspoons cold vegetable stock or water
4 teaspoons light sesame or peanut oil
1 large onion, chopped
8 cloves garlic, minced
2 teaspoons grated peeled fresh ginger
1 cup diced or diagonally sliced carrot
1 cup diced turnip
1 cup diced peeled celeriac or sliced celery
1 medium sweet potato, peeled and diced
4 cups sliced bok choy, with leaves
Salt to taste

Combine the tamari, Sucanat, sherry, and ¼ cup stock in a shallow bowl and stir together. Add the tempeh and marinate, refrigerated, for at least 20 to 30 minutes and up to 4 hours, turning it several times.

Combine the kuzu and cold stock in a small bowl and set it aside until the kuzu has dissolved, about 2 minutes.

Set a wok over medium heat. Add 2 teaspoons of the oil. Remove the tempeh from the marinade and add it to the wok, turning it immediately to coat both sides with oil. Brown the tempeh on both sides. Remove it from the pan and dice.

Add the remaining 2 teaspoons oil to the wok, swirling it to coat the bottom and sides. Add the onion and stir-fry for 2 to 3 minutes, until it appears translucent. Add the garlic and ginger, and continue stir-frying for several minutes, gradually adding the carrot, turnip, celeriac, and sweet potato. Stir in the diced tempeh, remaining marinade, and remaining 1 cup stock. Bring the liquid just to a boil, then cover the wok and reduce the heat. Simmer gently, stirring occasionally, for about 10 minutes or until the vegetables are tender.

Add the bok choy and dissolved kuzu. Cook, stirring, until the sauce thickens and the bok choy leaves are still bright green. Season with salt if needed and serve immediately.

Serves 4

Calories: 331   Total fat: 8 g   Protein: 14 g
Carbohydrates: 47 g   Cholesterol: 0 g   Sodium: 1192 mg

Tangy Tempeh with Portobello Mushrooms

Tempeh, portobello mushrooms, and miso contribute a "meaty" heartiness to this dish, and balsamic vinegar provides a bit of tang. Serve this sumptuous stew-like sauce over a cooked grain—a mixture of long-grain rice with kasha or wild rice is one of my favorites—or on pasta or egg noodles.

2 teaspoons light sesame or canola oil
1 8-ounce package tempeh
4 teaspoons extra-virgin olive oil
2 medium red onions, sliced lengthwise
*   into thin crescents*
4 to 8 cloves garlic, minced
4 portobello mushrooms, 3 to 4 inches in
*   diameter, stems and caps sliced*
*   separately*
¾ cup vegetable stock
1 tablespoon dark barley miso
1 tablespoon mellow barley miso
¼ cup balsamic vinegar
Freshly ground black pepper to taste
2 tablespoons minced fresh parsley
2 tablespoons minced fresh basil (optional)

Set a wok over medium heat and add the sesame or canola oil. Add the tempeh, turn it to coat both sides with oil, and brown it well. Remove the tempeh from the wok and cut it into strips about 1½ inches long and ¼ to ½ inch wide.

Set the wok over medium-high heat. Pour the olive oil around the rim and tilt the pan to coat the sides. Add the onion and stir-fry for 2 to 3 minutes. Add the garlic and sliced mushroom stems and continue stir-frying for about 2 minutes. Add the sliced mushroom caps and stir-fry until moistened.

Add all but 2 tablespoons of the stock and bring it to a simmer. Cook, stirring often, for several minutes, until the vegetables are tender and the stock has reduced by about half. Reduce the heat to medium-low.

Whisk together the misos and balsamic vinegar. Whisk in the remaining 2 tablespoons stock. Add this mixture to the wok. Season with black pepper. Stir in the parsley, and basil if desired, reserving a bit to sprinkle over each serving.

Serves 4

Calories: 269	Total fat: 11 g	Protein: 13 g
Carbohydrates: 28 g	Cholesterol: 0 g	Sodium: 61 mg

Tempeh Gremolata

Gremolata, a piquant mixture of lemon zest, minced fresh garlic, and parsley, enlivens this tempeh-vegetable stir-fry. Serve it over long-grain rice or pasta.

5 large cloves garlic, minced
1 teaspoon finely grated lemon zest
2 tablespoons minced fresh parsley
4 teaspoons extra-virgin olive oil
1 8-ounce package tempeh
1 large leek, white part only, halved
    lengthwise, sliced, and well rinsed
1 large carrot, sliced thin
2 cups thinly sliced fennel bulb
1 cup vegetable stock
¼ cup dry white wine
Freshly ground black pepper to taste
Salt to taste

In a small bowl, thoroughly mix 1 minced clove of garlic with the lemon zest and parsley; set aside.

Set a wok over medium-high heat and add 2 teaspoons of the oil. Add the tempeh and turn it immediately to coat both sides with oil. Brown on both sides. Remove the tempeh from the wok and cut it into strips about 1½ inches long and ¼ to ½ inch wide.

Add the remaining oil to the wok over medium-high heat. Add the leek, and stir-fry for about 1 minute. Add the remaining garlic and the carrot; continue stir-frying for about 2 minutes. Stir in the fennel and stir-fry for about 2 minutes longer. Add the tempeh strips, stock, and wine. Bring the liquid to a boil and simmer, stirring often, for 5 minutes or so, until the vegetables are tender and liquid has almost cooked away. Add the gremolata and toss thoroughly with the other ingredients. Season with black pepper and salt. Serve immediately.

Serves 4

Calories: 214   Total fat: 8 g   Protein: 10 g
Carbohydrates: 20 g   Cholesterol: 0 g   Sodium: 148 mg

Seitan Stir-Fry

Seitan contributes its satisfying chewy robustness to this one-dish meal. I like to serve this stir-fry over soba noodles—about ¾ pound for 4 servings—tossed with a bit of dark sesame or hot chile oil. It's also a tasty topping for rice or millet.

2 teaspoons kuzu powder
4 teaspoons cold vegetable stock or water
1½ teaspoons shoyu or natural soy sauce
1½ teaspoons fresh lemon juice
1 tablespoon peanut oil
1 large leek, white part only, thinly sliced
    and well rinsed, or 1 large onion,
    halved and sliced thin
4 to 6 cloves garlic, minced
1 large carrot, sliced
⅔ cup sliced daikon radish
1 cup sliced fresh shiitake mushroom caps
1 teaspoon grated peeled fresh ginger
½ pound traditionally seasoned seitan, cut
    into small chunks or thin strips
2 cups thinly sliced bok choy or Chinese
    cabbage
3 to 4 cups broccoli, cut into small florets
    and stems
1 cup seitan marinade (see note)
1 tablespoon toasted sesame seeds

Combine the kuzu and cold stock in a small bowl and set aside until the kuzu has dissolved, about 2 minutes. Whisk in the shoyu and lemon juice; set aside.

Set a wok over high heat. Pour the oil around the rim and swirl it to coat the pan. Add the leek and stir-fry for about 2 minutes. Continue stir-frying for several minutes, gradually adding the garlic, carrot, daikon, shiitakes, ginger, and seitan. When the vegetables are almost tender, add the bok choy, broccoli, and seitan marinade. Cover and steam briefly.

Stir in the kuzu mixture and cook just until the sauce thickens. Serve immediately, sprinkled with sesame seeds.

Serves 4

Variation: Substitute cremini or white button mushrooms for the shiitakes.

Note: If you substitute unseasoned seitan, use vegetable stock and add more garlic, ginger, and shoyu to taste.

Calories: 224	Total fat: 5 g	Protein: 23 g
Carbohydrates: 21 g	Cholesterol: 0 g	Sodium: 192 mg

Seitan and Sauerkraut

Serve this subtly sweet and sour combination over rice, kasha, or noodles. Stir-fried mustard greens and leeks are an agreeable accompaniment.

1 tablespoon light sesame or other
    vegetable oil
1 large onion, chopped
6 cloves garlic, minced or sliced thin
1 large apple, peeled, cored, and
    chopped coarse
Freshly ground black pepper to taste
6 tablespoons seitan marinade or
    vegetable stock
6 ounces traditionally seasoned seitan, cut
    into ½-inch dice
3 tablespoons dried currants
1½ cups drained sauerkraut, juice reserved
6 tablespoons sauerkraut juice
1½ teaspoons minced fresh dill **or**
    ¾ teaspoon dried

Set a wok over medium-high heat and add the oil, swirling it to coat the pan. Add the onion and stir-fry for 2 to 3 minutes, until translucent. Stir in the garlic and apple and continue stir-frying for 2 to 3 minutes. Season with pepper and stir-fry briefly.

Add the marinade and heat it to a simmer. Stir in the seitan, currants, sauerkraut, and sauerkraut juice, and simmer over low heat, stirring occasionally, for about 5 minutes or until the flavors are melded and the liquid has reduced somewhat. Add the dill during the final minute or two of cooking. Serve hot.

Serves 4

Calories: 188   Total fat: 4 g   Protein: 16 g
Carbohydrates: 22 g   Cholesterol: 0 g   Sodium: 589 mg

Seitan Pepper "Steak"

Use a combination of green, red, yellow, and/or orange bell peppers for a particularly colorful presentation. Serve this saucy stir-fry over long-grain rice, udon, or other noodles.

1 teaspoon kuzu powder
2 teaspoons cold vegetable stock or water
1 tablespoon peanut or canola oil
1 large onion, quartered lengthwise and
    sliced
4 large cloves garlic, minced
2 teaspoons grated peeled fresh ginger
1 large green or red bell pepper, cut into
    thin 1½-inch-long strips
½ pound traditionally seasoned seitan, cut
    into thin 1½-inch-long strips
1 cup vegetable stock
1 tablespoon rice vinegar
2 tablespoons shoyu or natural soy sauce
Freshly ground black pepper to taste
Salt to taste
2 scallions, sliced on a diagonal

Combine the kuzu and cold stock in a small bowl and set aside until dissolved, about 2 minutes.

Set a wok over high heat. Pour the oil around the rim and swirl it to coat the pan. Add the onion and stir-fry for about 2 minutes, until translucent. Add the garlic, ginger, and bell pepper and continue stir-frying for 3 to 4 minutes. Stir in the seitan.

Add the stock and bring it just to a boil. Simmer gently for about 5 minutes or until the vegetables are tender, flavors are blended, and liquid is reduced by about half.

Whisk the vinegar and shoyu with the dissolved kuzu. Add this mixture to the wok, stirring constantly, until the sauce thickens. Season with pepper to taste and add salt if needed. Garnish with the scallions.

Serves 4

Calories: 170	Total fat: 5 g	Protein: 21 g
Carbohydrates: 13 g	Cholesterol: 0 g	Sodium: 591 mg

Seitan Stew

Assuage cold-weather appetites with this hearty dish, accompanied by braised brussels sprouts and a crusty bread.

4 teaspoons canola oil
1 large onion, chopped
8 cloves garlic, minced
1 large carrot, diced
1 large turnip, diced
1 cup diced celeriac or sliced celery
4 medium potatoes, diced
Freshly ground black pepper to taste
Pinch of ground cloves
1 bay leaf
1 cup seitan marinade or vegetable stock
½ cup dry red wine
½ pound traditionally seasoned seitan, cut
    into ½-inch dice (see note)
2 teaspoons kuzu powder
4 teaspoons cold vegetable stock or water
2 tablespoons dark barley miso
¼ cup vegetable stock
2 tablespoons minced fresh parsley

Set a wok over high heat. Pour the oil around the rim and swirl it to coat the pan.

Add the onion and stir-fry for 2 to 3 minutes, until translucent. Continue to stir-fry, gradually adding the garlic, carrot, turnip, celeriac, and potatoes. Add some pepper, the cloves, and the bay leaf; stir-fry briefly.

Add the marinade, wine, and seitan. Bring to a simmer, then cover the wok, reduce the heat, and simmer gently for 10 to 15 minutes or until the vegetables are tender.

Meanwhile, combine the kuzu and cold stock in a small bowl and set aside until dissolved, about 2 minutes. Whisk in the miso and ¼ cup stock. Add this mixture to the wok and simmer, stirring, until the stew thickens. Serve hot, garnished with the parsley.

Serves 4

Note: If you substitute unseasoned seitan, add more miso or some salt if needed.

Calories: 370   Total fat: 5 g   Protein: 23 g
Carbohydrates: 49 g Cholesterol: 0 g   Sodium: 69 mg

Seitan Tzimmes

Tzimmes is a traditional Jewish stew, consisting of carrots, dried fruits, sweet spices, and sometimes beef. In Yiddish, *tzimmes* means "fuss," and it usually implies "making a mountain out of a molehill." The complex flavor of this savory stew definitely goes beyond the sum of its simple parts. Seitan adds substance, making this a satisfying main dish. I like to serve it with a combination of long-grain brown rice and wild rice.

1 tablespoon light sesame or canola oil
1 large onion, chopped
2 large carrots, chopped
2 medium sweet potatoes, peeled and diced
¼ teaspoon ground cinnamon
¼ teaspoon freshly grated nutmeg **or**
     ⅛ teaspoon ground
Freshly ground black pepper to taste
1 teaspoon grated peeled fresh ginger
½ teaspoon salt, plus more to taste
1½ cups seitan marinade, vegetable stock,
     or unsweetened apple or orange juice
½ pound traditionally seasoned seitan, cut
     into ½-inch dice
1 teaspoon finely grated orange zest
½ cup chopped pitted prunes
½ cup chopped unsulphured (preferably
     Turkish) apricots

Set a wok over medium-high heat. Pour the oil around the rim and swirl it to coat the pan. Add the onion and stir-fry about 3 minutes, until translucent. Add the carrots and continue stir-frying for about 3 minutes. Stir in the sweet potatoes, cinnamon, nutmeg, pepper, and ginger and stir-fry briefly.

Add ½ teaspoon salt and the marinade, seitan, zest, prunes, and apricots. Bring the liquid to a simmer. Cover the wok, reduce the heat, and simmer gently for about 10 minutes or until the vegetables are tender, liquid is reduced, and flavors are melded. Add more pepper and salt to taste.

Serves 4

Calories: 417	Total fat: 3 g	Protein: 22 g
Carbohydrates: 73 g	Cholesterol: 0 g	Sodium: 300 mg

6
GRAINS GALORE

Grains are the foundation of just about every ethnic cuisine—as well as the basis of a satisfying and healthful diet. As the recipes in this chapter illustrate, there's truly a whole world of grains to prepare in your wok or stir-fry pan: different rice varieties, plus wild rice, millet, barley, buckwheat, bulgur, and quinoa. Couscous is really a form of pasta, but I've included it here because most of us think of and use it more as a grain.

With some cooked grain on hand, you can have a one-dish meal from your wok in minutes. Asian fried rice is a classic example, but the possibilities are practically endless for quickly tossing leftover cooked grains together with vegetables, fruits, beans, nuts, and seasonings to create memorable combinations. Stir-Fried Lebanese Rice and Lentils puts a Middle Eastern spin on things. Quinoa, Bulgur, and Beans has a southwestern flair. Wild Rice and Chestnuts highlights midwestern fall flavors.

Try to plan ahead since cold grains work better than freshly cooked. Better yet, always make extra whenever you cook grains. Then you'll have the makings for these dishes at the ready for spur-of-the-moment planning.

Italian Arborio rice is one grain I like to cook from scratch in a wok. Risotto is a tremendously flexible format tastewise and is easy to improvise from just about any selection of vegetables and seasonings that congregate in the refrigerator. Use Risotto Primavera, Rooti-Kazooti Risotto, and New Year's Good Luck Risotto as springboards for your own experimentation. Spanish Rice, a paella-type Arborio rice preparation, is another welcome wokked grain dish.

Cajun Rice and Beans

This is a quick and easy way to pep up leftover rice and put together an out-of-the-ordinary one-dish dinner.

1 tablespoon extra-virgin olive oil
1 large onion, chopped fine
4 large cloves garlic, minced
1 cup finely diced celery
1 large green or red bell pepper, diced fine
Pinch of cayenne pepper or more to taste
Freshly ground black pepper to taste
4 cups cooked long-grain brown rice
    (page 151)
2 teaspoons minced fresh thyme
1 cup cooked red kidney beans (page 150)
1 tablespoon white wine vinegar or to taste
Salt to taste

Set a wok over medium-high heat. Pour the oil around the rim and swirl it to coat the inside of the pan. Add the onion and stir-fry for 2 to 3 minutes, until translucent. Add the garlic and continue stir-frying, gradually adding the celery and bell pepper. Season with cayenne and black pepper. Add the rice, thyme, beans, and vinegar and toss well. Heat the mixture, stirring, until it is warmed through. Season with salt.

Serves 4

Calories: 357   Total fat: 5 g   Protein: 9 g
Carbohydrates: 69 g   Cholesterol: 0 g   Sodium: 0 mg

Lebanese Rice and Lentils

Look for tiny French-style lentils that hold their shape well when cooked. If you have cooked lentils and rice on hand, this substantial, savory dish is quick to toss together. I like to serve it with whole wheat chapatis, tortillas, or pita and a colorful side dish, such as Gingery Kale and Crimson Cabbage (page 20) or Simple Sweet and Sour Cabbage (page 29).

2 teaspoons extra-virgin olive oil

1 large onion, chopped

4 cloves garlic, minced

1½ teaspoons ground cumin

2 ½ to 3 cups cooked green or brown lentils
    (page 150)

3 to 4 cups cooled cooked long-grain brown
    or brown basmati rice (page 151)

Freshly ground black pepper to taste

Salt to taste

½ cup finely chopped fresh mint

1 cup plain low-fat or soy yogurt, whisked

Set a wok over medium-high heat. Pour the oil around the rim and tilt the pan to coat the sides. Add the onion and stir-fry for 2 to 3 minutes, until translucent. Add the garlic and cumin; continue to cook briefly, stirring constantly. Stir in the cooked lentils and rice; toss until everything is hot. Season with pepper and salt. Mix in three-quarters of the mint. Garnish each serving with yogurt and a sprinkling of mint.

Serves 4 generously

Calories: 450   Total fat: 4 g   Protein: 19 g
Carbohydrates: 83 g   Cholesterol: 4 g   Sodium: 50 mg

Warm-Weather Couscous

This combination of summertime vegetables works well; substitute others in season.

1 cup raw couscous, preferably whole wheat
¼ teaspoon salt, plus more to taste
4 teaspoons extra-virgin olive oil
1½ cups boiling vegetable stock or water
½ teaspoon cumin seeds
½ teaspoon ground turmeric
¼ teaspoon coriander seeds
¼ teaspoon fennel seeds
¼ teaspoon caraway seeds
Pinch of cayenne pepper or to taste
1 medium red or yellow onion, chopped
4 cloves garlic, minced
1 cup diced peeled kohlrabi
1 large red, orange, or yellow bell pepper, sliced or diced
1½ cups tender young green or yellow wax beans or a combination, trimmed
2 cups sliced green or golden zucchini or other summer squash
1 medium to large tomato, diced
⅔ cup vegetable stock
2 tablespoons minced fresh cilantro or parsley
2 tablespoons dried currants
2 tablespoons coarsely chopped pistachios

Toss together the couscous and ¼ teaspoon salt in a bowl. Drizzle in 1 teaspoon of the oil, and stir until the couscous is evenly coated. Pour the boiling stock over the couscous, cover the bowl tightly, and set it aside for about 10 minutes.

Grind together the cumin, turmeric, coriander, fennel, caraway, and cayenne in a spice grinder or mortar and pestle; set aside.

Set a wok over medium-high heat, pour the remaining oil around the rim, and tilt the pan to coat the sides. Add the onion and stir-fry for 2 to 3 minutes, until translucent. Stir in the garlic and kohlrabi and continue stir-frying for 2 to 3 minutes. Gradually add the bell pepper, beans, and zucchini, stirring all the while.

Add the spice mixture and cook for about 1 minute longer, stirring constantly. Stir in the tomato and stock. Bring the liquid just to a simmer, cover the wok tightly, and cook for 5 to 10 minutes, until the vegetables are just tender. Add salt to taste.

Fluff the couscous and mound it on a platter or individual plates. Serve the vegetables on top, garnished with the cilantro, currants, and pistachios.

Serves 4

Calories: 289	Total fat: 7 g	Protein: 8 g
Carbohydrates: 48 g	Cholesterol: 0 g	Sodium: 303 mg

Cool-Season Couscous

My Algerian friend, Hadj, gave me a general outline for this traditional North African dish. Customarily it contains five vegetables and five spices, though there is a lot of leeway in the specific ingredients. Extra-virgin olive oil, onion, garlic, chickpeas or fava beans, dried fruits, and nuts are constants, but vegetables depend on the season. Lightly toasting the couscous in a dry skillet before soaking gives it an especially nutty flavor.

1 cup raw couscous, preferably whole wheat
¼ teaspoon salt, plus more to taste
4 teaspoons extra-virgin olive oil
1½ cups boiling vegetable stock or water
¼ teaspoon coriander seeds
¼ teaspoon fennel seeds
¼ teaspoon caraway seeds
½ teaspoon cumin seeds
½ teaspoon ground turmeric
Pinch of cayenne or to taste
1 medium onion, chopped
4 cloves garlic, minced
1½ cups thinly sliced green cabbage
1 medium carrot, sliced
1 medium sweet potato, peeled and diced
1 cup sliced fresh fennel bulb
1 cup cooked chickpeas (page 150) or fava beans (see note)
¾ cup bean cooking liquid or vegetable stock
2 cups well-rinsed coarsely chopped spinach leaves
2 scallions, chopped fine
2 tablespoons raisins
2 tablespoons coarsely chopped lightly toasted almonds
1 ripe pear, cored and sliced

Toss together the couscous and ¼ teaspoon salt in a bowl. Drizzle in 1 teaspoon of the oil and stir until the couscous is coated evenly. Pour the boiling stock over the couscous, cover the bowl tightly, and set it aside for about 10 minutes.

Grind together the coriander, fennel seeds, caraway seeds, cumin seeds, turmeric, and cayenne in a spice grinder or mortar and pestle; set aside.

Set a wok over medium-high heat and pour the remaining tablespoon of oil around the rim; tilt the pan to coat the sides. Add the onion and stir-fry for about 2 minutes, until translucent. Stir in the garlic and cabbage; continue stir-frying for 2 to 3 minutes, until the cabbage is wilted. Gradually add the carrot, sweet potato, and fennel, stirring all the while.

Add the spice mixture and cook about 1 minute longer, stirring constantly. Stir in the chickpeas and bean cooking liquid. Bring the liquid just to a simmer, cover the wok tightly, and cook for about 10 minutes, stirring occasionally, until the vegetables are tender. Stir in the spinach and add salt to taste.

Fluff the couscous and mound it on a platter or individual plates. Serve the vegetables on top, garnished with scallions, raisins, almonds, and pear slices.

Serves 4

Note: Use fresh fava beans if you can find them: they're incredibly delicious and little trouble to prepare. Just remove the beans from the large pods, lightly steam them, and then carefully slip each one out of its thick outer membrane.

Variation: Substitute a large leek, halved lengthwise, sliced, and well-rinsed, for the onion.

Calories: 402   Total fat: 7 g   Protein: 11 g
Carbohydrates: 71 g   Cholesterol: 0 g   Sodium: 344 mg

Wild Rice and Chestnuts

I like to serve this flavorful fluffy seasoned rice with baked sweet potatoes and steamed broccoli with lemon and sesame seeds or a simple green salad. It's also a splendid stuffing for large sweet bell peppers and baked winter squashes. Look for dried chestnuts in natural foods stores or in gourmet or Italian markets. Of course you may substitute fresh chestnuts for the dried ones—or use lightly toasted pine nuts.

½ cup dried chestnuts (see note)
1 tablespoon light sesame or extra-virgin
*   olive oil*
1 large onion, chopped fine
4 to 6 cloves garlic, minced
½ cup finely chopped carrot
½ cup finely chopped turnip
½ cup finely chopped parsnip
1 medium red bell pepper, chopped fine
½ teaspoon dried rosemary
1 teaspoon dried thyme
6 cups cooked wild rice (page 151)
Salt to taste
Freshly ground black pepper to taste
¼ cup minced fresh parsley

Soak the chestnuts for several hours or overnight in water to cover. In a small saucepan, simmer the soaked nuts until tender. Drain, saving the cooking water, and dice.

Set the wok over medium-high heat. Pour the oil around the rim and tilt the pan to coat the sides. Add the onion and stir-fry for 2 to 3 minutes, until translucent. Add the garlic and carrot and continue stir-frying, gradually adding the turnip, parsnip, and bell pepper. Add the rosemary and thyme and stir-fry for several minutes longer, until the vegetables are tender.

Add the rice and quickly toss it with the vegetables. Stir in the chopped chestnuts and 2 tablespoons of the reserved chestnut cooking water. Add the remaining stock if the rice is dry or sticking. Add salt and pepper to taste. Stir in the parsley and serve immediately.

Serves 4 generously

Note: If you use fresh chestnuts or pine nuts, substitute vegetable stock for the chestnut cooking water.

Calories: 424	Total fat: 6 g	Protein: 10 g
Carbohydrates: 82 g	Cholesterol: 0 g	Sodium: 466 mg

Fruited Tame and Wild Rice

This simply prepared grain dish makes a scrumptious centerpiece for an autumn or winter meal.

1 medium apple
1 medium pear
¼ cup fresh orange juice
1 tablespoon extra-virgin olive or
    light sesame oil
1 medium onion, chopped
2 large cloves garlic, minced
½ cup thinly sliced fennel bulb
1 teaspoon finely grated orange zest
½ cup chopped black mission figs
4 cups cooled cooked wild rice (page 151)
2 cups cooled cooked brown basmati rice
    (page 151)
2 teaspoons fresh lemon juice
¼ cup minced fresh parsley
½ cup coarsely chopped toasted walnuts or
    pecans
Salt to taste

Core the apple and pear and cut them into small dice; you should have about a cup of each. Add the orange juice and stir well to coat the fruit.

Set a wok over medium-high heat. Pour the oil around the rim and swirl it to coat the pan. Add the onion and stir-fry for 2 to 3 minutes, until translucent. Add the garlic and fennel and continue stir-frying for 2 to 3 minutes. Add the orange zest, chopped fruit and juice, figs, rices, and lemon juice. Toss all together well, then continue to stir-fry until the grains are hot. Stir in the parsley and nuts. Season with salt to taste.

Serves 4

Calories: 571   Total fat: 14 g   Protein: 11 g
Carbohydrates: 98 g   Cholesterol: 0 g   Sodium: 315 mg

Kasha Classic

This grain dish is a variation of traditional Jewish *kasha varnitchkes*, which combines sautéed onions, roasted buckwheat groats, and bow tie noodles. If you're using leftover kasha, you'll need 3 to 4 cups. For a more exotic flavor, substitute fresh shiitakes or another kind of mushroom—or use a combination.

1 tablespoon light sesame or canola oil
1 cup raw toasted buckwheat groats
Pinch of salt
1½ cups boiling mild vegetable stock or
    water
1 large onion, chopped
4 large cloves garlic, minced
½ pound cremini or white button
    mushrooms, stems and caps sliced
    separately
Freshly ground black pepper to taste
6 ounces rotini, farfalle, or other short cut
    of pasta, cooked al dente
1 tablespoon shoyu or natural soy sauce to
    taste
2 tablespoons minced fresh dill

Drizzle 1 teaspoon of the oil over the buckwheat groats in a 1½-quart saucepan and stir to coat the individual grains. Add the salt and boiling stock, and bring it just back to a boil. Cover, reduce the heat as low as possible, and cook for 15 minutes. Remove the pan from the heat, leaving the lid in place. Cool.

Set a wok over medium-high heat and pour the remaining oil around the rim; tilt the pan to coat the sides. Add the onion and stir-fry for 2 to 3 minutes, until translucent. Add the garlic and mushroom stems; continue stir-frying about 1 minute. Add the mushroom caps and stir-fry for 2 to 3 minutes longer, until the mushrooms appear moist and the onion is tender. Add some black pepper and remove the wok from the heat.

Fluff the kasha with a fork and add it to the wok along with the cooked pasta, 1 tablespoon shoyu, and the dill. Set over low to medium heat and toss until the mixture is warm. Taste and add more pepper and shoyu if needed.

Serves 4

Variation: For a more colorful dish, add a medium to large red, orange, or yellow bell pepper, cut into short, thin strips, to the stir-fry along with the garlic and mushroom stems.

Calories: 357	Total fat: 5 g	Protein: 9 g
Carbohydrates: 67 g	Cholesterol: 0 g	Sodium: 453 mg

Curried Rice

Serve this vibrant golden grain mixture on a bed of tender spinach leaves or mixed baby greens.

1 teaspoon cumin seeds
½ teaspoon coriander seeds
½ teaspoon ground turmeric
Pinch of ground cinnamon
Pinch of ground cardamom
Pinch of ground cloves
Pinch of ground fenugreek
Pinch of cayenne pepper
1 tablespoon light sesame or canola oil
1 large onion, chopped
4 large cloves garlic, minced
1 large carrot, halved lengthwise and sliced
    thin on a diagonal
1 medium fennel bulb, sliced thin
2 teaspoons grated peeled fresh ginger
½ teaspoon salt, plus more to taste
¼ cup vegetable stock
¼ cup raisins
½ cup green peas, fresh or frozen
4 cups cooked basmati rice (page 151)
1 tablespoon fresh lemon juice
Freshly ground black pepper to taste
½ cup chopped fresh cilantro
¼ cup coarsely chopped toasted cashews

Toast the cumin and coriander seeds separately in a dry heavy skillet over low to medium heat. Cool the seeds, then grind them together with the turmeric, cinnamon, cardamom, cloves, fenugreek, and cayenne, using a spice grinder or mortar and pestle.

Set a wok over medium-high heat. Pour the oil around the rim and swirl it to coat the pan. Add the onion and stir-fry for 2 to 3 minutes, until translucent. Add the garlic and continue stir-frying, gradually adding the carrot, fennel, and ginger. Add the spice mixture and stir-fry briefly. Add ½ teaspoon salt, the vegetable stock, and the raisins. Cover the wok, reduce the heat, and steam for several minutes, until the vegetables are tender and the raisins plumped.

Add the peas and rice and toss all together until everything is well mixed and heated through. Add the lemon juice and black pepper and toss again. Season with more salt if needed. Stir in the cilantro and cashews and serve immediately.

Serves 4

Calories: 377	Total fat: 8 g	Protein: 7 g
Carbohydrates: 68 g	Cholesterol: 0 g	Sodium: 315 mg

Millet and Winter Squash Medley

Subtle spicing enhances the natural sweetness of millet and squash in this light autumn or winter grain dish. Add some lightly toasted pine nuts for an extra-special touch.

1 tablespoon sesame oil

1 medium to large sweet onion, chopped
    fine

4 cloves garlic, minced

¼ cup chopped red bell pepper

2 cups diced peeled butternut squash

¼ teaspoon ground cumin

¼ teaspoon ground coriander

¼ teaspoon ground cinnamon

¼ teaspoon freshly grated nutmeg or
    ⅛ teaspoon ground

½ cup vegetable stock

½ teaspoon salt, plus more to taste

4 cups cooked millet (page 151)

1 teaspoon fresh lemon juice or more to
    taste

Freshly ground black pepper to taste

¼ cup minced fresh parsley

Set a wok over medium-high heat. Pour the oil around the rim and swirl it to coat the pan. Add the onion and stir-fry for 2 to 3 minutes, or until translucent. Add the garlic and bell pepper and continue stir-frying for 2 to 3 minutes.

Stir in the squash, along with the cumin, coriander, cinnamon, and nutmeg; stir-fry briefly, taking care not to burn the spices. Add the stock and ½ teaspoon salt. Bring the liquid just to a simmer, cover the wok, reduce the heat, and simmer gently for 5 minutes or so, until the squash is tender.

Add the millet and lemon juice; toss with the vegetables and heat, stirring often. Add black pepper and the parsley; toss again. Taste and add more salt and/or lemon juice if needed.

Serves 4

Calories: 502	Total fat: 8 g	Protein: 13 g
Carbohydrates: 95 g	Cholesterol: 0 g	Sodium: 279 mg

Rooti-Kazooti Risotto

A wok works exceptionally well for making risotto, a creamy-textured Italian rice dish that requires a lot of simmering and stirring. Root vegetables and sweet potatoes give this particular version spots of warm-spectrum colors and a subtle sweetness.

1 tablespoon extra-virgin olive or light
    sesame oil
1 large leek, white and green parts kept
    separate, thinly sliced and well washed
4 to 8 large cloves garlic, minced
⅓ cup finely diced carrot
⅓ cup finely diced turnip
⅓ cup finely diced parsnip
⅓ cup finely diced rutabaga
⅓ cup finely diced sweet potato or
    garnet yam
Freshly ground black pepper to taste
1½ cups raw Arborio rice
½ teaspoon salt, plus more to taste
5½ to 6 cups hot vegetable stock
1 teaspoon minced fresh dill or
    ½ teaspoon dried
½ teaspoon minced fresh marjoram or
    ¼ teaspoon dried
1 tablespoon mellow barley miso
2 tablespoons minced fresh parsley

Set the wok over medium-high heat. Pour the oil around rim and tilt the pan to coat the sides. Add the white part of the leek and stir-fry for about 1 minute. Add the garlic to taste and stir-fry for about a minute longer. Gradually add the carrot, turnip, parsnip, rutabaga, and sweet potato, stir-frying briefly between additions. Add black pepper, the rice, and ½ teaspoon salt; stir-fry for about 1 minute.

Stir in 1½ cups of the stock and cook over medium heat, stirring often, until it is almost absorbed by the rice. Continue adding the stock, ½ cup at a time, stirring frequently until almost absorbed, reserving ¼ cup stock, and cooking the risotto for a total of 25 to 30 minutes, until the rice is creamy yet slightly firm in the center of each grain. In the last 5 minutes of cooking, stir in the green part of the leek, plus the dill and marjoram. Remove the wok from the heat.

Thoroughly mix the miso with the remaining ¼ cup stock, then stir it into the risotto. Taste and add more salt if needed. Serve immediately, garnished with the parsley.

Serves 4

Calories: 342	Total fat: 4 g	Protein: 6 g
Carbohydrates: 67 g	Cholesterol: 0 g	Sodium: 693 mg

New Year's Good Luck Risotto

Black-eyed peas are the lucky charm in this south-of-the-border-seasoned dish. Serve it with corn bread or tortillas and stir-fried greens for an auspicious beginning to the new year.

1 tablespoon extra-virgin olive oil
1 large onion, chopped fine
4 large cloves garlic, minced
Pinch cayenne pepper or 1 small fresh chile pepper, seeded and minced (optional, see note)
1 large red bell pepper, chopped
1½ cups Arborio rice
1 teaspoon ground cumin
½ teaspoon ground coriander
½ teaspoon salt, plus more to taste
5½ to 6 cups hot vegetable stock
2 cups cooked black-eyed peas (page 150)
1 tablespoon lime juice
1 medium avocado, peeled, pitted, and sliced or diced
2 tablespoons chopped fresh cilantro

Set a wok over medium-high heat. Pour the oil around the rim, then tilt the pan to coat the sides. Add the onion and stir-fry 2 to 3 minutes, until translucent. Add the garlic, cayenne, and bell pepper and continue stir-frying for 2 to 3 minutes. Stir in the rice, cumin, coriander, and ½ teaspoon salt; stir-fry for about 1 minute longer.

Add 1½ cups of the stock and cook over medium heat, stirring often, until it is almost absorbed by the rice. Continue adding stock ½ cup at a time, stirring frequently, for 25 to 30 minutes, until the rice is creamy yet firm in the center of each grain. Stir in the black-eyed peas, lime juice, and additional salt to taste. Remove the wok from the heat. Serve the risotto immediately, topped with the avocado and cilantro.

Serves 4

Note: If you leave out the chile or cayenne, provide a raw or cooked red or green salsa for everyone to add to taste.

Calories: 430	Total fat: 10 g	Protein: 12 g
Carbohydrates: 69 g	Cholesterol: 0 g	Sodium: 681 mg

Risotto Primavera

Leeks are at their best after they've wintered over, and tender spinach, radishes, and peas are some of the earliest spring garden vegetables. Combine them all with creamy Arborio rice for a sumptuous supper.

2 teaspoons extra-virgin olive oil
1 large leek, white part only, halved length-
*   wise, sliced, and well rinsed*
4 cloves garlic, minced
1½ cups Arborio rice
½ teaspoon salt, plus more to taste
5½ to 6 cups hot vegetable stock
4 red radishes, halved lengthwise and
*   sliced thin*
½ pound well-rinsed chopped
*   spinach leaves*
¼ cup fresh or frozen green peas
2 tablespoons fresh lemon juice

Set a wok over medium-high heat. Pour in the oil and tilt the pan to coat the sides. Add the leek and stir-fry about 1 minute. Add the garlic and rice; continue stir-frying for 1 to 2 minutes. Reduce the heat to medium.

Stir in ½ teaspoon salt and 1½ cups of the stock. Simmer, stirring often, until the liquid is almost absorbed by the rice. Continue adding stock ½ cup at a time, stirring frequently, for about 25 to 30 minutes or until the rice is creamy yet slightly firm in the center of each grain.

Stir in the radishes, spinach, peas, and lemon juice. Add more salt to taste. Remove the risotto from the heat and serve immediately.

Serves 4

Variation: Substitute snow peas, sliced into strips on a diagonal, for the green peas.

Calories: 224	Total fat: 2 g	Protein: 5 g
Carbohydrates: 44 g	Cholesterol: 0 g	Sodium: 322 mg

Barley and Mushroom "Risotto"

Cooked barley gives this hearty, earthy-flavored dish a creamy consistency similar to that of risotto.

1 quart boiling water
1 ounce dried shiitake mushrooms
1 tablespoon light sesame or extra-virgin
*   olive oil*
1 large onion, chopped
8 large cloves garlic, minced
1 cup thinly sliced carrot
1 pound cremini mushrooms, caps and
*   stems sliced separately*
4 cups cooked barley (page 151)
1 tablespoon shoyu or natural soy sauce
2 tablespoons mellow barley miso
2 tablespoons minced fresh dill
2 tablespoons minced fresh parsley
Salt to taste

Pour the boiling water over the shiitakes. Set aside for at least 30 minutes, until the mushrooms are reconstituted. Drain, reserving the soaking water. Remove the shiitake stems and discard. Thinly slice the caps. Heat the reserved stock; you should have at least 3½ cups.

Set a wok over medium-high heat. Pour the oil around the rim and swirl it to coat the pan. Add the onion and stir-fry for 2 to 3 minutes, until translucent. Add the garlic and carrot and continue stir-frying 2 to 3 minutes longer. Stir in the sliced shiitakes. Gradually add the fresh mushrooms, stirring constantly.

Add the barley and about 1½ cups of the hot stock. Simmer, stirring often, until the liquid is mostly absorbed. Gradually add 1½ cups more stock, about ½ cup at a time, stirring frequently. When most of the stock has been absorbed and the mixture reaches a somewhat creamy consistency, reduce the heat to low and stir in the shoyu.

Whisk together the miso and ¼ cup of the remaining shiitake stock. Stir this and half the minced herbs into the wok mixture. Season with salt to taste. Serve immediately, garnished with the remaining herbs.

Serves 4

Variation: If you make this in late spring, add several tender asparagus spears, sliced thin on a diagonal, close to the end of cooking.

Calories: 321   Total fat: 3 g   Protein: 8 g
Carbohydrates: 61 g   Cholesterol: 0 g   Sodium: 285 mg

Mediterranean Rice

A quick makeover transforms plain rice into an exciting accompaniment for Colorful Caponata (page 25), Rainbow Peppers and Red Onion (page 32), and other Mediterranean-style dishes.

1 tablespoon extra-virgin olive oil
1 medium to large onion, chopped fine
4 large cloves garlic, minced
Freshly ground black pepper to taste
¼ cup dried currants
½ cup vegetable stock
½ teaspoon salt, plus more to taste
4 cups cooled cooked long-grain brown rice
*   (page 151)*
2 tablespoons fresh lemon juice
¼ cup minced fresh mint leaves
¼ cup lightly toasted pine nuts

Set a wok over medium-high heat. Pour the oil around the rim, and swirl it to coat the inside. Add the onion and stir-fry for 2 to 3 minutes, until translucent. Stir in the garlic and continue stir-frying for 2 to 3 minutes, until the onion is just tender. Grind in black pepper and stir in the currants.

Add the stock and bring it to a simmer. Add the salt and rice and cook, stirring often, until the grain is heated through. Add the lemon juice, mint, and pine nuts; toss well. Taste and add more pepper and salt if needed.

Serves 4

Calories: 366   Total fat: 9 g   Protein: 8 g
Carbohydrates: 64 g   Cholesterol: 0 g   Sodium: 270 mg

Quinoa, Bulgur, and Beans

Prepare the grains in advance and toss together dinner in a jiffy. Serve this quick, satisfying dish with stir-fried greens and a fruit salsa.

½ cup quinoa, well rinsed and drained
½ cup coarse bulgur
¼ teaspoon salt, plus more to taste
1½ cups boiling water
1 tablespoon light sesame or peanut oil
1 medium onion, chopped fine
4 large cloves garlic, minced
Minced fresh chile pepper to taste
1 medium red bell pepper, chopped fine
1 teaspoon ground cumin
1 cup cooked corn kernels
1 cup cooked black (turtle) beans
    (page 150)
¼ cup toasted pumpkin seeds (page 27)
2 scallions, sliced thin
3 to 4 teaspoons fresh lime juice
1 medium avocado, peeled, pitted, and
    sliced or diced (optional)
Chopped fresh cilantro (optional)

Combine the quinoa and bulgur in a medium saucepan over low heat. Toast the grains lightly, stirring often. Add ¼ teaspoon salt and the boiling water and bring it just to a boil. Stir once, tightly cover the pan, and reduce the heat as low as possible. Cook for 15 minutes, then remove the pan from the heat, leaving its lid in place. Cool to room temperature.

Set a wok over medium-high heat. Add the oil and swirl it to coat the inside of the pan. Add the onion and stir-fry for 2 to 3 minutes, until translucent. Add the garlic, chile, and bell pepper; continue to stir-fry for several minutes, until the vegetables are tender. Add the cumin and stir-fry briefly. Add the corn, beans, and grain mixture; toss thoroughly. Add the pumpkin seeds, scallions, and 3 teaspoons lime juice; toss again. Mix in more lime juice and salt as needed. Serve immediately, garnished with avocado and cilantro if desired.

Serves 4

Calories: 440	Total fat: 11 g	Protein: 17 g
Carbohydrates: 66 g	Cholesterol: 0 g	Sodium: 147 mg

French Flavors Rice

This quick vegetable and rice combo makes a one-dish meal. For a more saladlike effect and a slightly sharper flavor, leave the arugula out of the stir-fry and ring the plates with it.

1 tablespoon extra-virgin olive oil
1 large onion, chopped
4 large cloves garlic, minced
1 large carrot, sliced
½ pound cremini or white button mushrooms, sliced thick
1 cup tender young green beans or sugar snap peas, trimmed
2 to 4 small tender zucchini, preferably golden, halved lengthwise and sliced on a diagonal (about 1 cup)
½ teaspoon salt, plus more to taste
¼ cup dry white wine
4 cups cooled cooked long-grain brown rice (page 151)
1 tablespoon fresh lemon juice
2 tablespoons minced fresh tarragon **or** *2 teaspoons dried*
¼ cup minced fresh parsley
Freshly ground black pepper to taste
4 cups coarsely chopped arugula

Set a wok over medium-high heat. Pour the oil around the rim and swirl it to coat the sides. Add the onion and stir-fry for about 3 minutes, until translucent. Add the garlic and carrot and continue stir-frying for about 3 minutes. Gradually add the mushrooms, beans, and zucchini, stirring constantly.

Add ½ teaspoon salt and the wine. Bring the wine to a simmer, then cover the vegetables with the rice. Cover the wok, reduce the heat slightly, and steam for several minutes, until the vegetables are tender and the rice is heated through.

Add the lemon juice, tarragon, and parsley. Grind in some black pepper. Toss thoroughly. Season with more salt to taste. Add the arugula and toss again. Serve immediately.

Serves 4

Calories: 351	Total fat: 5 g	Protein: 8 g
Carbohydrates: 67 g	Cholesterol: 0 g	Sodium: 297 mg

Spanish Rice

Here's an all-vegetable version of Spain's traditional rice dish, paella. Italian Arborio rice is similar to the starchy medium-grain rice customarily used in Spain. By all means substitute a Spanish variety if you can find it. If you like, dress up this dish with more vegetables: green beans, peas, summer squash, or eggplant.

1 tablespoon extra-virgin olive oil
1 large onion, chopped
4 large cloves garlic, minced
1 green or red bell pepper, diced
½ teaspoon minced fresh thyme **or**
    ¼ teaspoon dried
½ teaspoon minced fresh rosemary **or**
    ¼ teaspoon dried
Cayenne pepper or hot red pepper flakes to
    taste
½ teaspoon sweet paprika
1 cup peeled (page 151) diced tomatoes
1½ cups Arborio rice
3½ to 4 cups vegetable stock
1 teaspoon salt, plus more to taste
¼ teaspoon crushed saffron threads
Freshly ground black pepper to taste
2 tablespoons minced fresh parsley
Chopped pitted green olives (optional)

Set a wok over medium-high heat. Pour the oil around the rim and swirl it to coat the inside of the pan. Add the onion and stir-fry for 2 to 3 minutes, until translucent. Add the garlic and bell pepper and continue stir-frying for about 3 minutes. Add the thyme, rosemary, cayenne, and paprika; stir-fry briefly. Stir in the tomatoes and simmer, stirring often, until most of the liquid cooks away.

Stir in the rice until it is coated with the tomato mixture. Add 3½ cups stock, 1 teaspoon salt, and the saffron. Bring to a simmer over medium-high heat and cook, uncovered, without stirring, for about 25 minutes, gradually reducing the heat to low. If the rice isn't done, add more stock and continue cooking for another 10 to 15 minutes.

Remove the pan from the heat and cover it with a kitchen towel for about 10 minutes. Season with black pepper and add more salt if needed. Serve garnished with the parsley and olives to taste if desired.

Serves 4

Calories: 233   Total fat: 2 g   Protein: 4 g
Carbohydrates: 44 g   Cholesterol: 0 g   Sodium: 543 mg

Thai Fried Rice

This is a pleasant blend of hot, tart, and sweet—and with a good measure of crunch. Adjust the amount of chile to suit your own taste.

1 tablespoon peanut oil
1 medium to large onion, chopped
4 large cloves garlic, minced
1 fresh or dried red Thai chile, minced
1 teaspoon grated peeled fresh ginger
1 cup thinly sliced carrot
1 cup thinly sliced red bell pepper
2 cups thinly sliced Chinese cabbage
4 cups cold cooked jasmine rice (page 151)
½ cup finely grated fresh coconut
2 tablespoons fresh lime juice
2 to 3 tablespoons shoyu or natural
    soy sauce
½ cup chopped fresh cilantro
¼ cup chopped dry-roasted peanuts

Set a wok over medium-high heat. Pour the oil around the rim and swirl it to coat the inside of the pan. Add the onion and stir-fry for 2 to 3 minutes, until translucent. Add the garlic, chile, ginger, and carrot and continue stir-frying, gradually adding the bell pepper and cabbage.

When the vegetables are tender, add the rice and stir-fry until heated through. Add the coconut, lime juice, 2 tablespoons shoyu, the cilantro, and the peanuts and toss well. Taste and add more shoyu if needed.

Serves 4

Calories: 392	Total fat: 16 g	Protein: 8 g
Carbohydrates: 51 g	Cholesterol: 0 g	Sodium: 688 mg

7
Oodles of Noodles

Some of the world's greatest cuisines feature noodles in one or more of their many guises. Italian pastas alone vary from long ribbons to "rice" kernels and everything in between, though they all derive from the noodles Marco Polo supposedly brought back to Italy from the East centuries ago. Then there's the large roster of Asian noodles, composed of wheat, rice, or buckwheat. Noodles are a favorite food around the world, and an international selection has inspired the recipes in this chapter.

Take your own cook's tour of noodle dishes from your wok. Relish rustic Pasta e Fagioli one evening; go for Spicy Chinese Nutty Noodles the next. Curried Capellini conjures up India, and Lemony Greek Orzo will transport you to the Mediterranean. Noodle and vegetable combinations are practically limitless.

Like grains, noodles are terrific starting points for quick-fix one-dish meals. Cook the noodles in a big pot of boiling water while you stir-fry a select group of vegetables and seasonings. Add the drained noodles to the wok, adjust the seasonings, and voilà! Dinner is served.

Broccoli-Almond Udon

This colorful, quick dish has a lot of appealing crunch.

1 tablespoon peanut oil
2 teaspoons minced garlic
1 cup thinly sliced carrot
1 cup thinly sliced daikon radish
1 cup thinly sliced red bell pepper
2 teaspoons grated peeled fresh ginger
1 cup diagonally sliced scallion
½ cup vegetable stock
4 cups small broccoli florets
Freshly ground black pepper to taste
¾ pound udon, cooked (see note)
¼ cup shoyu or natural soy sauce
Several shakes dark sesame oil
½ cup lightly toasted almonds,
      chopped coarse
Salt to taste

Set a wok over medium-high to high heat. Pour the peanut oil around the rim and swirl it to coat the pan. Add the garlic and carrot and stir-fry for 1 to 2 minutes. Continue to stir-fry, gradually adding the daikon, bell pepper, ginger, and scallion.

Add the stock and broccoli and continue stir-frying until the vegetables are tender, the broccoli is still bright green, and most of the liquid has cooked away. Add black pepper, the cooked noodles, shoyu, and sesame oil. Stir everything together. Mix in the almonds. Taste and add salt if needed. Serve immediately.

Serves 4

Note: To cook udon, place the uncooked noodles in a pot of rapidly boiling water; when the water returns to a boil, add about 1 cup of cold water. Return to a boil and add another cup of cold water; repeat until the noodles are tender throughout, about 10 minutes altogether.

Calories: 430   Total fat: 12 g   Protein: 11 g
Carbohydrates: 65 g   Cholesterol: 0 g   Sodium: 1713 mg

Linguine with Leeks and Greens

A wok easily accommodates the large volume of uncooked greens that go into this pleasing pasta dish. Piquant escarole and arugula accented by pungent garlic, capers, and Greek olives and balanced with sweet raisins and pine nuts provide a satisfying symphony of flavors.

1 tablespoon extra-virgin olive oil
1 large leek, halved lengthwise, sliced thin,
*   and well rinsed*
6 to 8 cloves garlic, minced
1 large bunch (about ¾ pound) escarole,
*   chopped coarse*
¼ cup raisins, preferably golden
2 tablespoons capers
¼ cup chopped pitted kalamata olives
3 to 4 cups coarsely chopped arugula leaves
¼ cup chopped fresh parsley
¼ cup lightly toasted pine nuts, chopped
*   lightly toasted walnuts, or almonds*
¾ pound linguine, cooked al dente
Freshly ground black pepper to taste
Salt to taste

Set a wok over medium-high heat. Pour the oil around the rim and tilt the pan to coat the sides. Add the leek and stir-fry for about 1 minute. Add the garlic and continue to stir-fry for about 3 minutes as you gradually add the escarole.

Stir in the raisins, capers, and olives. Add the arugula, parsley, pine nuts, and pasta; quickly toss with the other ingredients. Remove from the heat and season with pepper and salt. Serve immediately.

Serves 4

Calories: 498   Total fat: 11 g   Protein: 14 g
Carbohydrates: 81 g   Cholesterol: 0 g   Sodium: 380 mg

Pasta e Fagioli

This herby version of pasta with beans makes an especially quick one-dish meal. If you can't find cannellini, substitute navy or great northern beans.

1 tablespoon extra-virgin olive oil
1 large red onion, chopped
4 large cloves garlic, minced
1 large carrot, sliced thin
1 cup thinly sliced fennel bulb
2 to 3 teaspoons minced fresh sage **or**
    1 teaspoon crushed dried
1 to 1½ teaspoons minced fresh thyme **or** ½
    teaspoon dried
Freshly ground black pepper to taste
½ teaspoon salt, plus more to taste
1½ cups bean cooking liquid or
    vegetable stock
3 cups cooked cannellini beans (page 150)
¾ pound fusilli or other short cut of pasta,
    cooked al dente
2 tablespoons minced fresh basil
4 cups well-rinsed coarsely chopped spinach
    or arugula leaves
1 tablespoon fresh lemon juice
2 tablespoons minced fresh parsley
Grated fresh Parmigiano Reggiano
    (optional)

Set a wok over medium-high heat. Pour the oil around the rim and swirl it to coat the pan. Add the onion and stir-fry for 2 to 3 minutes, until translucent. Add the garlic and continue stir-frying, gradually adding the carrot, fennel, sage, and thyme. Grind in black pepper. Add ½ teaspoon salt and the stock and bring to a simmer. Cover and simmer gently for several minutes, until the vegetables are tender.

Stir in the beans and simmer briefly. Add the pasta, basil, spinach, and lemon juice. Toss well and heat, stirring, until the spinach just wilts but is still bright green. Season with more salt and pepper to taste. Serve immediately, garnished with the parsley, and cheese if desired.

Serves 4

| Calories: 504 | Total fat: 5 g | Protein: 19 g |
| Carbohydrates: 95 g | Cholesterol: 0 g | Sodium: 328 mg |

Lemony Greek Orzo

Rice-shaped pasta, called orzo, is sometimes cooked in the same manner as Italian risotto, by gradually adding warm stock as the small grains absorb it. For a fluffier result, cook it in a large pot of rapidly boiling water just as you would other types of pasta.

1 tablespoon extra-virgin olive or
   canola oil
1 large red onion, chopped
8 cloves garlic, minced or sliced thin
1 large carrot, roll-cut (page 9) into
   thin slices
1 medium red bell pepper, sliced into short
   thin strips
3 cups small cauliflower florets
Freshly ground black pepper to taste
2 teaspoons minced fresh oregano or
   1 teaspoon dried
½ teaspoon salt, plus more to taste
½ cup vegetable stock
1⅓ cups orzo, cooked al dente
1 tablespoon fresh lemon juice
12 to 16 pitted kalamata olives, pitted and
   chopped
4 cups well-rinsed coarsely chopped spinach
   leaves
1 tablespoon umeboshi vinegar
¼ cup chopped fresh parsley
8 cherry tomatoes, quartered (optional)

Set a wok over medium-high heat. Pour the oil around the rim and swirl it to coat the pan. Add the onion and stir-fry about 2 minutes, until translucent. Add the garlic and cook briefly, stirring constantly. Gradually add the carrot, bell pepper, and cauliflower and continue to stir-fry for several minutes. Add black pepper and the oregano and stir-fry briefly.

Add ½ teaspoon salt and the stock. Bring to a simmer, cover the pan, and steam the vegetables, stirring occasionally. When the vegetables are tender and the stock has almost cooked away, add the orzo. Stir in the lemon juice, olives, spinach, and umeboshi vinegar; cook briefly, until the spinach is just wilted but still bright green. Taste and add more black pepper and salt if needed. Serve immediately, garnished with the parsley, and the tomatoes if desired.

Serves 4

Calories: 316   Total fat: 9 g   Protein: 8 g
Carbohydrates: 50 g   Cholesterol: 0 g   Sodium: 686 mg

Double Spinach Fettucine

You don't have to hunt down spinach fettuccine if it's not readily available; this creamy spinach sauce works perfectly well with plain fettuccine—and other forms of pasta, too.

1 tablespoon kuzu powder
2 tablespoons cold vegetable stock or water
2 cups low-fat milk or soy milk
2 tablespoons mellow white miso
1 tablespoon extra-virgin olive oil
1 large onion, finely chopped
4 to 6 large cloves garlic, minced
*1 large carrot, halved lengthwise and sliced
    thin on a diagonal*
½ teaspoon freshly grated nutmeg **or**
    ¼ teaspoon ground
Freshly ground black pepper to taste
1 tablespoon minced fresh tarragon **or**
    1 teaspoon dried
*½ pound fresh spinach leaves, well rinsed
    and chopped*
4 teaspoons fresh lemon juice
¼ cup minced fresh parsley
*¾ to 1 pound spinach fettucine, cooked
    al dente*
¼ cup chopped pitted kalamata olives
Salt to taste

Combine the kuzu and cold stock in a small bowl and set aside until the kuzu is dissolved, about 2 minutes. Add ⅓ to ½ cup of the milk and the miso. Whisk until the mixture is smooth.

Set a wok over medium-high heat. Add the oil and swirl it to coat the pan. Add the onion and stir-fry for 2 to 3 minutes, until translucent. Add the garlic and carrot; continue to stir-fry 3 to 4 minutes, until the carrot is just tender. Add the nutmeg, black pepper, and tarragon; stir-fry briefly. Stir in the remaining milk and heat, but do not boil.

Reduce the heat to low and stir in the kuzu-miso mixture. Cook, stirring, until the sauce thickens. Stir in the spinach and lemon juice; cook, stirring, until the spinach wilts but is still bright green. Stir in the parsley, pasta, and olives. Season with salt and serve immediately.

Serves 4

Calories: 497	Total fat: 9 g	Protein: 22 g
Carbohydrates: 80 g	Cholesterol: 5 g	Sodium: 315 mg

Magnificent Magenta Pasta

The pasta turns a vibrant color that will knock your socks off! For a quick one-dish meal, serve it ringed with mixed baby greens.

1 tablespoon extra-virgin olive oil
1 large sweet red onion, chopped
6 to 8 cloves garlic, minced
Freshly ground black pepper to taste
2 cups thinly sliced beet greens (optional)
¼ cup dried currants
4 medium beets, cooked (reserve ¾ cup cooking liquid), peeled, and cut into thin 1½-inch-long strips
½ teaspoon salt, plus more to taste
½ cup dry red wine
¾ pound farfalle or other short cut of pasta, cooked al dente
2 tablespoons fresh lemon juice
2 tablespoons minced fresh dill or 1 tablespoon dried
¼ cup lightly toasted pine nuts

Set a wok over medium-high heat. Pour the oil around the rim and swirl it to coat the pan. Add the onion and stir-fry for 2 to 3 minutes, or until translucent. Stir in the garlic and continue stir-frying for about 1 minute. Grind in pepper, add the beet greens if desired, and stir-fry for about 2 minutes, until the greens wilt.

Stir in the currants, beets, and salt. Add the wine and reserved beet cooking liquid and bring it to a simmer. Cook, stirring often, for several minutes, until the vegetables are thoroughly tender and the liquid is considerably reduced.

Add the cooked pasta and lemon juice and toss well. Season with more salt and pepper. Add the dill and pine nuts; toss again and serve immediately.

Serves 4

Calories: 424	Total fat: 7 g	Protein: 11 g
Carbohydrates: 67 g	Cholesterol: 0 g	Sodium: 299 mg

Penne with Asparagus and Tarragon—Mustard Sauce

Whisk together this piquant sauce in the wok, cook the pasta and asparagus together, and voilà—a wonderful springtime entree.

4 cloves garlic, minced
1½ to 1¾ cups vegetable stock
Freshly ground black pepper to taste
1½ tablespoons Dijon mustard
3 tablespoons tahini (sesame paste)
1 tablespoon fresh lemon juice
1 tablespoon minced fresh tarragon or 1½
*   teaspoons dried, or more to taste*
3 to 4 tablespoons capers
Salt to taste
¾ pound penne or other short cut of pasta
8 to 12 good-sized asparagus stalks, peeled
*   and cut ¼ to ½ inch long on a*
*   diagonal*
2 to 3 tablespoons minced fresh chives
4 to 6 cups well-rinsed coarsely chopped
*   tender spinach or arugula leaves*

Bring a large pot of water to a boil for cooking the penne.

Combine the garlic and 1½ cups stock in a wok; bring to a simmer, cover, lower the heat, and simmer gently for about 5 minutes. Grind in some pepper and remove the wok from the heat.

In a small bowl, whisk together the mustard, tahini, and several tablespoons of the hot stock. Whisk this mixture into the stock in the wok and bring to a gentle simmer over low heat, whisking constantly for several minutes, until it thickens. Add more stock, a tablespoon at a time, if the sauce requires thinning. Whisk in the lemon juice, tarragon, and capers to taste. Taste and season with more pepper and salt if needed. Simmer the sauce briefly, then remove it from the heat.

Add a pinch of salt and the penne to rapidly boiling water and cook until al dente. Stir in the asparagus, then immediately drain. Add the pasta and asparagus to the wok and toss with the sauce. Add chives to taste and toss again. Divide the greens among four plates and top with the pasta and sauce.

Serves 4

Calories: 345	Total fat: 7 g	Protein: 11 g
Carbohydrates: 58 g	Cholesterol: 0 g	Sodium: 598 mg

Spicy Chinese Nutty Noodles

A wok is an especially good place to toss together and warm ingredients at the same time. Serve this colorful, brightly flavored dish as part of a light supper, lunch, or brunch.

1 large egg
Pinch salt
3 teaspoons light sesame oil
1 teaspoon hot chile oil
2 teaspoons minced garlic
3 tablespoons shoyu or natural soy sauce
4 teaspoons rice vinegar
4 scallions, sliced thin
½ cup red bell pepper, cut into thin
*   1-inch-long strips*
½ pound thin spaghetti
2 cups broccoli, cut into small florets
*   and stems*
¼ cup finely chopped unsalted dry-roasted
*   peanuts*
¼ cup chopped fresh cilantro

Beat the egg with the salt. Set a wok over medium heat. Add 1 teaspoon of the sesame oil and swirl it to coat the sides of the pan. Add the beaten egg and tilt the wok to spread it thinly. As the egg cooks, loosen the edge with a spatula. Remove the wok from the heat. Fold the egg sheet into thirds, transfer it to a cutting board, and slice it into thin strips.

Whisk the remaining 2 teaspoons of sesame oil with the hot chile oil, garlic, shoyu, and vinegar. Add this mixture to the wok over low heat, along with the scallions and bell pepper.

Cook the spaghetti in rapidly boiling water. When it is just about done, add the broccoli. Cook for about 1 minute more and drain.

Add the pasta and broccoli to the wok. Add the peanuts and toss with the other ingredients. Heat briefly, stirring often, until everything is warmed through. Add the cilantro and toss again. Serve immediately, garnished with egg shreds.

Serves 4 modestly

Calories: 328	Total fat: 11 g	Protein: 12 g
Carbohydrates: 45 g	Cholesterol: 53 g	Sodium: 805 mg

Curried Capellini

*S*avor these spicy, coconut milk–coated fine noodles with flashes of red, orange, and bright green. Substitute a thicker noodle if you prefer.

1 tablespoon peanut oil
1 medium to large sweet onion, chopped
8 cloves garlic, minced
½ red jalapeño chile, seeded and minced, or to taste
1 large carrot, julienned
1 medium to large red bell pepper, cut to match the carrot
1 teaspoon grated peeled fresh ginger
1 tablespoon lightly toasted Sri Lankan curry powder (see note)
1 teaspoon ground turmeric
1 cup vegetable stock
1 cup coconut milk
2 tablespoons fresh lime juice
2 tablespoons shoyu or natural soy sauce
1 pound capellini, cooked al dente
Salt to taste
4 to 6 cups well-rinsed coarsely chopped spinach leaves
4 red radishes, cut into matchsticks
¼ cup finely chopped unsalted dry-roasted peanuts
½ cup chopped fresh cilantro or ¼ cup minced rau ram leaves (see Glossary)

Set a wok over high heat. Pour the oil around the rim and swirl it to coat the pan. Add the onion and stir-fry for about 2 minutes, until translucent. Gradually add the garlic, jalapeño, carrot, bell pepper, and ginger, continuing to stir-fry for several minutes. Add the curry powder and turmeric and stir-fry briefly.

Add the stock and bring to a simmer. Cook gently for several minutes, stirring often, until the vegetables are just tender. Add the coconut milk, lime juice, shoyu, and capellini. Stir gently over low heat until the noodles are warm and saturated with sauce. Season with salt.

Divide the spinach among four plates. Arrange the noodles on top, garnished with the radishes, peanuts, and cilantro. Serve immediately.

Serves 4

Note: I use a locally mixed lightly toasted Sri Lankan curry powder, composed of coriander, cumin, fennel, cardamom, Ceylon cinnamon, curry leaves, and spices. Prepare a similar blend or substitute your own favorite curry spice mixture.

Calories: 599	Total fat: 19 g	Protein: 16 g
Carbohydrates: 84 g	Cholesterol: 0 g	Sodium: 757 mg

Eastern European Paprika Noodles

Harried and hurried? Here's a hearty one-dish meal that will be on the table in minutes.

2 tablespoons mellow rice miso
¼ cup vegetable stock
1 tablespoon fresh lemon juice
4 teaspoons canola oil
1 large sweet onion, chopped
1 pound cremini or white button
    mushrooms, stems and caps
    sliced separately
4 cups thinly sliced green cabbage
Freshly ground black pepper to taste
½ teaspoon salt, plus more to taste
2 tablespoons minced fresh dill **or**
    2 teaspoons dried
1 tablespoon sweet paprika, plus more for
    topping
½ pound egg noodles, cooked until
    just tender
½ to 1 cup plain low-fat or soy yogurt
2 tablespoons minced fresh parsley

Whisk together the miso, stock, and lemon juice.

Set a wok over high heat. Pour the oil around the rim and swirl it to coat the sides. Add the onion and stir-fry for about 2 minutes, until translucent. Continue to stir-fry for about 5 minutes, gradually adding the mushroom stems and caps and the cabbage. Add black pepper, ½ teaspoon salt, the dill, 1 tablespoon paprika, and the noodles; toss gently. Stir in the miso mixture. Taste and add more salt and pepper if needed. Serve immediately, topped with yogurt, more paprika, and parsley.

Serves 4

| Calories: 357 | Total fat: 6 g | Protein: 12 g |
| Carbohydrates: 57 g | Cholesterol: 53 g | Sodium: 324 mg |

Shiitakes and Soba

This quick, one-dish meal offers lots of possibilities for improvisation: substitute other vegetables in season.

2 teaspoons kuzu powder
4 teaspoons cold vegetable stock or water
3 to 4 tablespoons shoyu or natural
    soy sauce
1 tablespoon peanut oil
8 scallions, sliced thin on a diagonal
4 large cloves garlic, minced
1 tablespoon grated peeled fresh ginger
1 large carrot, julienned
1 medium kohlrabi, peeled and julienned
½ cup julienned daikon radish
8 fresh shiitake mushrooms, stemmed and
    sliced thin
1 cup vegetable stock
6 to 8 cups well-rinsed coarsely chopped
    fresh spinach leaves
¾ pound soba noodles, cooked (see note)
2 teaspoons hot chile oil
½ cup chopped fresh cilantro

Combine the kuzu and cold stock in a small bowl and set aside for a few minutes, until dissolved. Whisk in 3 tablespoons of the shoyu.

Set a wok over high heat. Pour the peanut oil around the rim and swirl it to coat the pan. Add the scallions, garlic, and ginger and stir-fry briefly. Add the carrot and continue stir-frying, gradually adding the kohlrabi, daikon, and shiitakes.

Add the stock and bring it to a simmer. Cover the wok and steam briefly, until the vegetables are tender. Add the spinach, noodles, hot chile oil, and kuzu mixture. Stir gently until the sauce thickens and everything is heated through. Mix in the cilantro and add more shoyu to taste. Serve immediately.

Serves 4

Note: To cook the noodles evenly, bring a large pot of water to a rapid boil, add the noodles, and cook, stirring frequently, until the water returns to a boil; then add a cup of cold water to the pot. Repeat this process about two times more, or until the noodles are tender. Drain the noodles and immediately add them to the wok or plunge them into cold water and drain them again.

Calories: 501   Total fat: 12 g   Protein: 14 g
Carbohydrates: 83 g   Cholesterol: 0 g   Sodium: 1071 mg

Pasta al Greco

This pasta dish is rich and hearty yet quick to put together. Serve it with some crusty bread. Get a head start by soaking the tomatoes in advance; once they're cool, refrigerate them until you're ready to cook.

¾ cup (about 1½ ounces) sun-dried
    tomatoes
2 tablespoons extra-virgin olive oil
1 large red onion, sliced thin
6 large cloves garlic, minced
Freshly ground black pepper to taste
18 to 24 kalamata olives, pitted and sliced
2 to 3 tablespoons capers
¾ pound fusilli, farfalle, or other short cut
    of pasta, cooked al dente
¼ cup finely chopped fresh basil
¼ cup finely chopped fresh parsley
½ cup crumbled feta cheese (see variation)
6 to 8 cups coarsely chopped arugula

Cover the tomatoes with boiling water; set aside to soak until reconstituted. Drain, reserving the soaking water. Cut the tomatoes into thin strips.

Set a wok over medium-high heat. Pour in 4 teaspoons of the oil and swirl it to coat the pan. Add the onion and stir-fry for 2 to 3 minutes, until translucent. Add the garlic and black pepper and stir-fry briefly.

Stir in the sun-dried tomatoes along with 6 to 8 tablespoons of the reserved soaking water. Cover the wok, reduce the heat, and simmer for several minutes, until the onion and tomatoes are tender. Stir in the olives and capers. Add the pasta, the remaining 2 teaspoons oil, half the basil and parsley, and the feta; toss well. Remove from the heat.

Line four plates with the arugula. Top with the pasta mixture. Serve immediately, garnished with the remaining basil and parsley.

Serves 4

Variation: Press and lightly blanch or steam (page 152) 6 ounces tofu; cool, then slice and marinate in a mixture of 1½ tablespoons fresh lemon juice and 1 tablespoon umeboshi vinegar. Substitute for the feta.

Calories: 529   Total fat: 19 g   Protein: 14 g
Carbohydrates: 69 g   Cholesterol: 25 g   Sodium: 1084 mg

Farfalle with Fennel and Arugula

This piquant main dish, combining sliced red onion and fennel bulb with pasta butterflies or bows in an orange-balsamic vinaigrette, all laced with sage, derives from one of my favorite winter salads. Use a fruity-flavored fresh sage if you can find it. Toss in some pomegranate seeds at the end for an extra-festive color and flavor touch.

1 teaspoon kuzu powder
2 teaspoons cold water
2 teaspoons prepared stone-ground mustard
½ cup fresh orange juice
¼ cup balsamic vinegar
1 teaspoon salt or to taste
4 cups arugula, torn into bite-sized pieces
4 teaspoons extra-virgin olive oil
1 large red onion, sliced lengthwise into
    thin crescents
4 large cloves garlic, minced
2 cups thinly sliced fennel bulb
2 tablespoons minced fresh sage or
    2 teaspoons dried
¾ pound farfalle, cooked al dente
Freshly ground black pepper, to taste
1 navel orange, peeled and sectioned

Combine the kuzu and water in a small bowl and set aside until dissolved, about 2 minutes. Whisk in the mustard, orange juice, balsamic vinegar, and 1 teaspoon salt.

Divide the arugula among four large plates.

Set the wok over medium-high heat. Pour the oil around the rim and swirl it to coat the pan. Add the onion and stir-fry for about 2 minutes. Gradually add the garlic, fennel, and sage and continue stir-frying for several minutes, until the fennel is crisp-tender. Add the cooked pasta and toss well.

Reduce the heat to medium-low and pour in the orange juice mixture. Stir gently but constantly until the ingredients are coated evenly with slightly thickened sauce. Season with black pepper. Add more salt if needed. Serve immediately on the arugula and garnish each serving with a few orange sections.

Serves 4

Calories: 354   Total fat: 6 g   Protein: 9 g
Carbohydrates: 65 g   Cholesterol: 0 g   Sodium: 665 mg

Egg Noodles with Apricots and Almonds

I like to use thin (about ¼-inch-wide) twisted egg noodles for this dish, but other kinds will work as well. Arugula's pungency nicely complements the apricots' and almonds' sweetness.

1⅓ cups boiling water
½ cup slivered unsulphured dried apricots
1 tablespoon light sesame or other vegetable
    or nut oil
1 large onion, chopped fine
¼ teaspoon ground coriander
¼ teaspoon ground cinnamon
¼ teaspoon grated fresh nutmeg **or**
    ⅛ teaspoon ground
Freshly ground black pepper to taste
½ teaspoon salt, plus more to taste
½ pound egg noodles, cooked until just
    tender
2 teaspoons fresh lemon juice
½ cup lightly toasted slivered almonds
½ cup minced fresh parsley
4 cups coarsely chopped arugula leaves

Pour the boiling water over the apricots; cover and set aside for 20 to 30 minutes, until they have softened and cooled.

Set a wok over medium-high heat. Pour the oil around the rim and swirl it to coat the pan. Add the onion and stir-fry for 4 to 5 minutes, until golden and tender. Add the coriander, cinnamon, nutmeg, and pepper and stir-fry briefly, taking care not to burn the spices. Stir in the apricots with their soaking liquid and ½ teaspoon salt. Reduce the heat to low and add the cooked noodles, lemon juice, almonds, and three-quarters of the parsley; toss everything together. Taste and season with more salt if needed.

Divide the arugula among four plates and top with the noodle mixture. Sprinkle the remaining parsley on top.

Serves 4

Calories: 408   Total fat: 13 g   Protein: 11 g
Carbohydrates: 57 g   Cholesterol: 50 g   Sodium: 282 mg

Red Pepper and Pear Pasta

This quick pasta dish—with a refreshing Asian taste twist—is perfect for autumn, when fall fruits mix with the late-summer vegetable harvest.

1 tablespoon peanut or canola oil
1 large onion, sliced into thin crescents
4 large cloves garlic, minced
1 large carrot, sliced thin
2 large red bell peppers, cut into thin strips
2 teaspoons grated peeled fresh ginger
2 medium tomatoes, sliced thin
2 large ripe pears, peeled, cored, and
  sliced thin
Freshly ground black pepper to taste
Salt to taste
¾ to 1 pound thin spaghetti, linguine, or
  udon, cooked al dente
2 tablespoons minced fresh cilantro

Set a wok over high heat. Pour the oil around the rim and swirl it to coat the pan. Add the onion and stir-fry for 2 to 3 minutes, until translucent. Add the garlic and carrot and stir-fry for about 2 minutes. Add the bell peppers and ginger; continue to stir-fry for 2 to 3 minutes, until the vegetables are tender.

Add the tomatoes and pears and cook, stirring, for about 3 minutes. Season with pepper and salt. Add the pasta and toss with the sauce. Serve immediately, garnished with the cilantro.

Serves 4

Calories: 482   Total fat: 4 g   Protein: 14 g
Carbohydrates: 95 g   Cholesterol: 0 g   Sodium: 26 mg

Corn Twists with Collards and Black-Eyed Peas

Now you can have your pasta and down-home, southern-style cooking all at the same time. Lime juice, cilantro, and pumpkin seeds add a southwestern dimension to this dish. I use multicolored vegetable-dyed corn twists that hold together well after cooking, but any corn pasta, preferably a short cut, will do.

1½ tablespoons mellow barley miso
3 tablespoons bean cooking liquid or
*   vegetable stock*
1½ to 2 tablespoons fresh lime juice
1 tablespoon extra-virgin olive oil
1 large onion, chopped fine
6 large cloves garlic, minced
1 large red bell pepper, diced fine
5 cups collard greens, finely chopped leaves
*   and thinly sliced stalks kept separate*
1½ teaspoons cumin seeds, lightly toasted
*   and ground*
Pinch cayenne pepper or more to taste
2 cups cooked black-eyed peas (page 150)
8 to 9 ounces corn twists, cooked al dente
Salt to taste
½ cup chopped fresh cilantro
3 tablespoons lightly toasted pumpkin seeds
*   (page 27)*

Combine the miso, bean cooking liquid, and 1½ tablespoons of the lime juice in a small mixing bowl and whisk together; set aside.

Set a wok over medium-high heat and add the oil; tilt the pan to coat the sides. Add the onion and stir-fry for 2 to 3 minutes, until translucent. Add the garlic and bell pepper and continue stir-frying for about 2 minutes. Add the sliced collard stems, cumin, and cayenne; stir-fry for about 1 minute longer. Stir in the collard leaves and stir-fry for a minute or two more, until the leaves and other vegetables are tender. Reduce the heat to low.

Add the peas, pasta, and miso mixture and toss everything together. Taste and add salt and/or more lime juice if needed. Add the cilantro and pumpkin seeds and toss again. Serve immediately.

Serves 4

Calories: 805	Total fat: 8 g	Protein: 15 g
Carbohydrates: 85 g	Cholesterol: 0 g	Sodium: 48 mg

Cavatelli with Onions, Cabbage, and Currants

Here's a quick-to-fix, satisfying supper dish. Use green or red cabbage—or a combination—as you please.

2 teaspoons canola oil
2 teaspoons extra-virgin olive oil
2 large sweet onions, sliced thin
8 to 12 cloves garlic, minced
6 cups thinly sliced cabbage
¼ cup dried currants
¼ cup dry red wine
¾ pound cavatelli or other short cut
    of pasta, cooked al dente
2 teaspoons fresh lemon juice
Salt to taste
Freshly ground black pepper to taste
¼ cup chopped fresh parsley

Set a wok over medium-high heat and add both oils; tilt the pan to coat the sides. Add the onions and stir-fry for 2 to 3 minutes, until translucent. Add the garlic to taste and continue stir-frying for 5 to 10 minutes, until the vegetables are soft and sweet tasting.

Gradually add the cabbage, stirring all the while. Stir-fry for 3 to 5 minutes, until the cabbage is wilted. Add the currants and wine. Stir-fry for 3 to 5 minutes longer, until the currants are soft and cabbage is tender.

Add the cooked pasta and lemon juice to the wok and toss everything together. Season with salt and pepper. Add the parsley. Toss again and serve immediately.

Serves 4

Calories: 399   Total fat: 5 g   Protein: 10 g
Carbohydrates: 73 g   Cholesterol: 0 g   Sodium: 29 mg

Rotini with a Thai Twist

This is a takeoff on pad Thai, Americans' favorite Thai noodle dish.

¼ cup shoyu or natural soy sauce

¼ cup fresh lime juice

2 teaspoons Sucanat or light brown sugar

2 teaspoons tamarind concentrate
  (see Glossary)

1 tablespoon peanut oil

1 large carrot, sliced thin

4 cloves garlic, minced

1 fresh hot chile, seeded and minced,
  or to taste

2 teaspoons grated peeled fresh ginger

1 medium red bell pepper, sliced thin

4 scallions, sliced on a diagonal

2 cups mung bean sprouts

4 cups thinly sliced Chinese cabbage
  or bok choy

¾ pound rotini, cooked al dente

2 eggs, lightly beaten

½ cup finely chopped dry-roasted peanuts

½ cup chopped fresh cilantro

Salt to taste

Whisk together the shoyu, lime juice, Sucanat, and tamarind; set aside.

Set a wok over high heat. Pour the oil around the rim and swirl it to coat the pan. Add the carrot and stir-fry for about 2 minutes. Add the garlic, chile, ginger, and bell pepper and stir-fry for 1 to 2 minutes, or until the carrot and pepper are tender. Add the scallions, sprouts, cabbage, and rotini; toss together and continue stir-frying until everything is hot.

Drizzle in the egg, stirring constantly. Stir in the shoyu mixture, peanuts, and cilantro. Taste and add salt if needed. Serve immediately.

Serves 4

Calories: 563   Total fat: 15 g   Protein: 21 g
Carbohydrates: 83 g   Cholesterol: 107 g   Sodium: 1310 mg

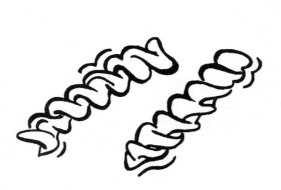

8

SIMPLE SAUCES AND CLASSY CONDIMENTS

Have you ever felt frustrated when whisking a sauce in a saucepan or skillet? You're sure to find it's much easier in a round-bottomed wok or stir-fry pan, because the curved surface provides consistent contact between the whisk and every smidgen of sauce. Pan shape and size also furnish the option of making a lot or a little, as you wish. Chutneys and the like take well to canning and are handy to have on hand both for enhancing everyday meals and as special additions to impromptu international feasts.

This modest selection of sauces complements many other dishes in the book. Cranberry Chutney has holiday written all over it, and Ruby Red Raspberry Applesauce spells cozy comfort. Great Green Tomato Hot Sauce adds gusto to southwestern and south-of-the-border specialties, and Onion and Currant Confit especially perks up Italian meals. Nectarine Ketchup is a terrific topping for the wontons in the next chapter, Spicy Peanut Sauce an integral part of the Indonesian Peanutty Pockets. Get out your wok and whisk and go to it!

Cranberry Chutney

Add this colorful condiment to your cold-weather holiday feasts.

1⅓ cups apple cider or unsweetened
    apple juice
½ cup finely diced unsulphured
    dried apricots
¼ cup maple syrup
3 cups fresh cranberries
2 medium apples, peeled, cored, and
    diced fine
1 teaspoon finely grated orange zest
1 teaspoon grated peeled fresh ginger
Pinch of salt or to taste
Pinch of cayenne pepper or to taste
2 tablespoons fresh lemon juice
Fresh orange juice as needed

Heat the cider just to boiling in a wok. Add the apricots and maple syrup. Cover, reduce the heat, and simmer for about 5 minutes or until the fruit is almost tender.

Add the cranberries, apples, orange zest, ginger, salt, and cayenne. Simmer for 5 to 10 minutes longer, until the berries and apples are tender. Stir in the lemon juice. Thin to the desired consistency with several tablespoons of orange juice. Serve at room temperature or chilled. Refrigerate leftovers in an airtight jar.

Makes about 3 cups

Per ¼-cup serving:
Calories: 70
Carbohydrates: 17 g
Total fat: 0 g
Cholesterol: 0 g
Protein: 0 g
Sodium: 0 mg

Piquant Pear Chutney

Lemon zest and juice and vinegar subtly balance the sweet components of this condiment, a delightful accompaniment to curries, dal, and other Indian-style dishes. Multiply the ingredients to make a larger amount—it's a welcome gift. Tightly covered and refrigerated, it will keep for several weeks; you can also preserve it by canning.

1 medium onion, chopped fine
4 large pears, peeled, cored, and diced
2 teaspoons finely grated lemon zest
2 tablespoons fresh lemon juice
½ cup unsweetened apple juice or cider
2 tablespoons apple cider vinegar
2 teaspoons grated peeled fresh ginger
⅔ cup chopped dried figs
2 tablespoons Sucanat or light brown sugar
¼ teaspoon ground allspice
¼ teaspoon ground cinnamon
Minced fresh chile or cayenne pepper
    to taste
¼ teaspoon salt or to taste

Combine all the ingredients in a wok set over medium-high heat and bring to a simmer. Reduce the heat and cook gently, uncovered, stirring occasionally, for about 45 minutes to an hour or until the onion is tender and the mixture reaches the desired thickness. Serve at room temperature or chilled. Refrigerate leftovers in an airtight jar.

Makes about 3 cups

Per ¼-cup serving:
Calories: 101   Total fat: 0 g   Protein: 1 g
Carbohydrates: 23 g   Cholesterol: 0 g   Sodium: 48 mg

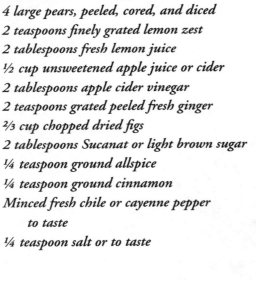

Gingered Tomato Chutney

Here's the perfect condiment to perk up many different sorts of meals. Try it with your next Indian feast—or serve it on veggie burgers.

1 medium onion, chopped

1 pound tomatoes, peeled (page 151) and diced

1 teaspoon minced garlic

1½ teaspoons grated peeled fresh ginger

1 tablespoon Sucanat or light brown sugar

2 tablespoons cider vinegar

Pinch of cayenne or to taste

Pinch of ground coriander or to taste

Pinch of salt or to taste

¼ cup golden raisins

Combine all the ingredients in a wok set over medium heat. Bring to a simmer, cover, and cook gently, adjusting the heat as necessary, for 30 to 45 minutes or until the sauce reaches the desired consistency. If too much liquid remains, cook uncovered for several minutes. Serve at room temperature or chilled. Refrigerate leftovers in an airtight jar.

Makes about 2 cups

Per ¼-cup serving:

Calories: 41	Total fat: 0 g	Protein: 1 g
Carbohydrates: 9 g	Cholesterol: 0 g	Sodium: 7 mg

Onion and Currant Confit

Long-cooked onions and garlic take on a decidedly sweet character, especially when simmered with apple cider and currants. Balsamic vinegar rounds out the flavor of this versatile relish. Try it on crusty bread.

6 cups thinly sliced sweet onion
6 large cloves garlic, minced
1 cup apple cider
½ teaspoon salt, plus more to taste
¼ cup dried currants
4 teaspoons balsamic vinegar

Combine the onion, garlic, cider, ½ teaspoon salt, and currants in a wok set over low to moderate heat. Cook 30 to 40 minutes, stirring often, until the onions are super-tender and sweet flavored.

Add the balsamic vinegar and cook for 5 to 10 minutes longer. Season with more salt. Remove from the heat, cover, and cool. Serve at room temperature or chilled. Refrigerate leftovers in an airtight jar.

Makes about 2 cups

Per ¼-cup serving:
Calories: 65   Total fat: 0 g   Protein: 1 g
Carbohydrates: 14 g   Cholesterol: 0 g   Sodium: 137 mg

Quick-Cook Peach Salsa

Serve this almost-instant fruity summer condiment with your next Mexican- or Indian-style meal. Don't add the peaches to the salsa too far in advance; their color and flavor are most vibrant when fresh.

2 teaspoons light sesame or canola oil
1 small to medium onion, chopped fine
2 cloves garlic, minced
2 small fresh red chiles, seeded and minced,
*   or to taste*
2 teaspoons grated peeled fresh ginger
4 medium peaches, peeled (page 151),
*   pitted, and diced fine*
4 teaspoons fresh lime juice
Salt to taste
2 tablespoons chopped fresh cilantro

Set a wok over medium-high heat. Add the oil and swirl it to coat the bottom of the pan. Add the onion and stir-fry for 2 to 3 minutes, until translucent. Add the garlic, chiles, and ginger and continue stir-frying for about 1 minute. Remove the wok from the heat and transfer the contents to a mixing bowl.

Stir in the peaches, lime juice, and salt. When the mixture is cool, add the cilantro. Serve immediately. Refrigerate leftovers in an airtight jar.

Makes about 3 cups

Per ½-cup serving:
Calories: 35   Total fat: 0 g   Protein: 0 g
Carbohydrates: 7g   Cholesterol: 0 g   Sodium: 1 mg

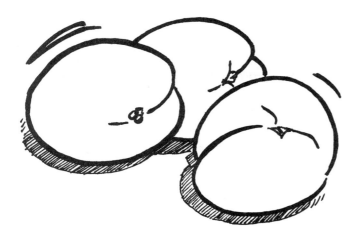

Good Gravy

Try this savory sauce over kasha or another cooked grain. For a heartier topping, add some seasoned sautéed mushrooms, tofu, or tempeh.

2 tablespoons light sesame oil
1 medium onion, chopped fine
4 cloves garlic, minced
¼ cup flour, preferably whole wheat pastry
    or brown rice flour
1 teaspoon dried sage
1 teaspoon dried thyme
3 cups cold vegetable stock
2 tablespoons shoyu or natural soy sauce
¼ cup minced fresh parsley
Salt to taste
Freshly ground black pepper to taste

Set a wok over medium-high heat. Add the oil and swirl it to coat the bottom of the pan. Add the onion and stir-fry for about 3 minutes, until translucent. Stir in the garlic and stir-fry for 2 to 3 minutes longer.

Sprinkle in the flour and herbs. Reduce the heat and cook, stirring, for 1 to 2 minutes or until the flour is absorbed and fragrant. Remove the wok from the heat for several minutes to cool the mixture.

Set the wok over medium heat. Gradually add the stock, whisking constantly. Bring the mixture to a boil, then reduce the heat and simmer gently, stirring occasionally, for about 15 minutes or until it reaches the desired consistency.

Add the shoyu, parsley, and salt and pepper to taste. Simmer briefly and serve. Refrigerate leftovers in an airtight container.

Makes about 3 cups

Variation: Substitute 2 to 3 teaspoons each minced fresh sage and thyme for the dried herbs. Add fresh herbs near the end of cooking.

Per ½-cup serving:
Calories: 84   Total fat: 4 g   Protein: 2 g
Carbohydrates: 8 g   Cholesterol: 0 g   Sodium: 592 mg

Great Green Tomato Hot Sauce

Gather up the green tomatoes in your garden before the first fall frost and preserve their tart taste in this spirited sauce. I especially like to use green plum tomatoes. This recipe makes a modest amount, but your wok will likely hold much more; just increase the quantities and cooking time accordingly. Serve this with tacos, fajitas, or any Mexican-style dish.

1 tablespoon extra-virgin olive oil
1 small onion, chopped
2 large cloves garlic, minced
1 small jalapeño chile, seeded and minced,
    or to taste
1 pound green tomatoes, diced fine
Freshly ground black pepper to taste
¼ teaspoon salt, plus more to taste
1 tablespoon apple cider vinegar
¼ cup chopped fresh cilantro

Set a wok over medium-high heat. Pour the oil around the rim and swirl it to coat the pan. Add the onion and stir-fry for 2 to 3 minutes, until translucent. Add the garlic and jalapeño and stir-fry briefly. Gradually add the tomatoes. Grind in black pepper and add ¼ teaspoon salt. Cover the wok, reduce the heat, and cook for 10 to 15 minutes, stirring often, until the tomato is tender.

Transfer the tomato mixture to a food processor or blender. Add the vinegar and cilantro. Process briefly, maintaining a somewhat coarse texture. Taste and add more pepper and salt as needed and serve. Refrigerate leftovers in an airtight container.

Makes about 2 cups

Per ¼-cup serving:
Calories: 35   Total fat: 1 g   Protein: 1 g
Carbohydrates: 8 g   Cholesterol: 0 g   Sodium: 146 mg

Spicy Peanut Sauce

This sauce is easy to whisk together in a wok. Adjust the hotness—amount of chile—to your taste. Use it for Indonesian Peanutty Pockets (page 145), as a topping for tofu or tempeh, or to top raw or steamed vegetables.

½ teaspoon peanut oil
2 large cloves garlic, minced
½ teaspoon grated peeled fresh ginger
1 fresh or dried Thai red pepper, seeded
    and minced
1 cup coconut milk or vegetable stock
½ cup chunky unsalted peanut butter
1 tablespoon fresh lime juice
2 teaspoons tamarind concentrate
    (see Glossary)
1 teaspoon Sucanat or light brown sugar
2 teaspoons shoyu or natural soy sauce

Set a wok over medium heat and add the oil, garlic, ginger, and pepper and stir-fry briefly. Add the coconut milk and heat gently. Gradually whisk in the peanut butter to a smooth consistency. Add the lime juice, tamarind, Sucanat, and shoyu, whisking until smooth. Remove from the heat and serve warm or at room temperature. Refrigerate leftovers in an airtight container.

Makes about 1¾ cups

Per ¼-cup serving:
Calories: 194   Total fat: 15 g   Protein: 6 g
Carbohydrates: 6 g   Cholesterol: 0 g   Sodium: 115 mg

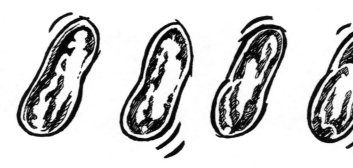

Creamy Cashew-Ginger Sauce

This rich-tasting sauce is a terrific topping for noodles, grains, and raw or cooked vegetables.

1 tablespoon peanut oil
1 large onion, chopped fine
2 large cloves garlic, minced
2 teaspoons grated peeled fresh ginger
Freshly ground black pepper to taste
1 cup roasted cashew butter
3 cups vegetable stock or water
1 tablespoon fresh lemon juice
2 tablespoons shoyu or natural soy sauce
Salt to taste

Set a wok over high heat. Pour the oil around the rim and swirl it to coat the pan. Add the onion and stir-fry for about 2 minutes, until translucent. Add the garlic and ginger and continue stir-frying for 2 to 3 minutes, or until the onion is tender. Add pepper and stir-fry briefly.

Lower the heat and add the cashew butter. Gradually incorporate the stock, stirring constantly. Add the lemon juice and shoyu and simmer gently over low heat, stirring often, until the sauce thickens to the desired consistency. Season with salt and serve. Refrigerate leftovers in an airtight container.

Makes about 3 cups

Per ¼-cup serving:
Calories: 150   Total fat: 11 g   Protein: 4 g
Carbohydrates: 8 g   Cholesterol: 0 g   Sodium: 248 mg

Ruby Red Raspberry Applesauce

The color—and flavor—of this simple sauce is glorious! Make it in the early autumn when apples and raspberries are both in season.

2½ pounds apples, cored and diced
½ cup apple cider or unsweetened
*   apple juice*
1 cup fresh red raspberries

Combine the apples and cider in a wok over medium-high heat. When the liquid comes to a simmer, cover the wok and reduce the heat to low. Cook, stirring occasionally, for about 20 minutes or until the apples are tender. Add the raspberries and remove the wok from the heat. Leave it covered for 5 to 10 minutes.

Put the fruit mixture through a food mill or sieve to remove the apple peels and raspberry seeds. Serve the sauce warm, at room temperature, or chilled. Refrigerate leftovers in an airtight container.

Makes 1 quart

Per ½-cup serving:

Calories: 98	Total fat: 0 g	Protein: 0 g
Carbohydrates: 23 g	Cholesterol: 0 g	Sodium: 1 mg

Nectarine Ketchup

Though ketchup is generally synonymous with tomatoes, the base of this thick, smooth sweet-and-sour sauce can just as easily be another succulent fruit.

4 medium nectarines, peeled (page 151), pitted, and chopped
1 cup finely chopped onion
4 large cloves garlic, minced
2 teaspoons grated peeled fresh ginger
½ cup water
½ cup Sucanat or light brown sugar
½ cup white wine vinegar
1 teaspoon salt

Combine all the ingredients in a wok and set over medium-high heat. Bring to a simmer. Reduce the heat and simmer gently for about 30 minutes. Remove from heat and let cool somewhat.

Blend briefly in a food processor or blender until the mixture is smooth. Serve warm or at room temperature. Refrigerate leftovers in an airtight container.

Makes about 2 cups

Per ¼-cup serving:
Calories: 84
Carbohydrates: 9 g
Total fat: 0 g
Cholesterol: 0 g
Protein: 0 g
Sodium: 135 mg

Dumpling Dipping Sauce

This is a classic soy-ginger sauce for Asian-style dumplings and steamed buns. For a really simple meal, you could also toss it with cooked noodles, garnished with extra scallions and some chopped cilantro.

2 teaspoons dark sesame oil or hot chile oil
¼ cup shoyu or natural soy sauce
2 teaspoons Sucanat or light brown sugar
2 teaspoons grated peeled fresh ginger
½ cup vegetable stock
4 teaspoons rice vinegar
¼ cup finely chopped scallions

Whisk together the oil, shoyu, Sucanat, ginger, stock, and vinegar in a wok set over medium heat. Bring just to a simmer. Stir in the scallions. Reduce the heat and simmer gently for several minutes, until the flavors are melded. Serve at room temperature. Refrigerate leftovers in an airtight container.

Makes about 1 cup

Per ¼-cup serving:

Calories: 40	Total fat: 2 g	Protein: 0 g
Carbohydrates: 4 g	Cholesterol: 0 g	Sodium: 1030 mg

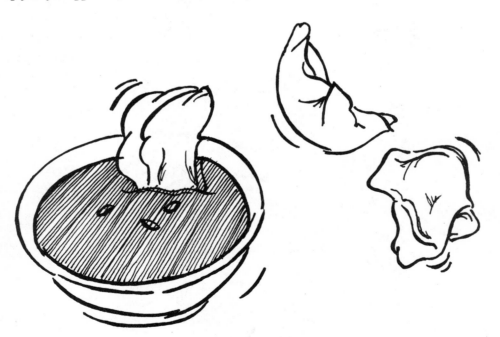

9
It's a Wrap

It's time to wrap up—and there are lots of ways to do it. Every culture seems to have some kind of stuffed bread, pastry, or pancake. I've come up with a few ideas to include here. Keep in mind that many other dishes in the book make splendid substitute stuffings.

It's perfectly acceptable to mix up wrappers and fillings: Indian chapatis, Middle Eastern pita and lavosh, and Norwegian lefse are just as good for holding Mexican taco fillings as their customary stuffings, and the reverse is true of tortillas. Have fun pairing different wrappers and fillings.

Mushroom-Stuffed Steamed Buns and Delectable Dumplings are slightly different formats, but the flexibility principle for fillings still applies. When you take the time to make a batch of either, make extra to freeze for future treats.

If you keep pliable flat breads on hand, you'll be ready to put together a quick meal or snack on a moment's notice. Flat breads and pitas freeze well and thaw almost instantly. Insert wax paper squares between breads before you freeze them so you can easily take out one at a time. I find all kinds of wrappers are easiest to manipulate and taste best when warmed. Steam breads briefly or wrap them in foil and heat for a few minutes in a moderate oven.

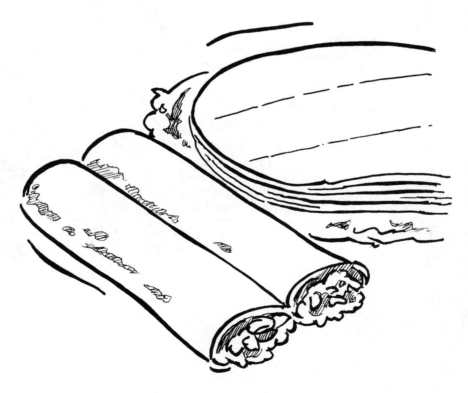

Seitan Fakin' Fajitas

Thinly sliced marinated seitan is a perfect substitute for the skirt steak strips commonly used for fajitas, and a wok is a good way to sear them. For a hearty meal, serve the fajitas with rice, refried beans, and steamed or stir-fried greens.

½ pound traditionally seasoned seitan, cut into thin, 3-inch-long strips

4 cloves garlic, minced

¼ cup fresh lime juice

1 tablespoon extra-virgin olive oil

1 medium to large onion, quartered and sliced thin

1 medium to large green or red bell pepper, sliced into thin strips

1 teaspoon ground cumin

Freshly ground black pepper to taste

¼ cup vegetable stock

4 large flour tortillas, warmed

Green or red salsa to taste

1 ripe avocado, peeled, pitted, and sliced thin

¼ cup coarsely chopped cilantro

Combine the seitan strips, garlic, and lime juice in a shallow bowl. Stir to coat, then refrigerate for several hours, stirring occasionally.

Steam the tortillas until soft, then wrap in an unnapped towel to keep them warm.

Set a wok over medium-high heat. Pour the oil around the rim and swirl it to coat the pan. Add the onion and stir-fry for 2 to 3 minutes, until translucent. Add the bell pepper, cumin, and black pepper and continue stir-frying for about 3 minutes. Add the marinated seitan and stir-fry for several minutes. Add the stock and continue to stir-fry until the liquid has almost cooked away.

Spoon a quarter of the seitan mixture down the middle of each tortilla, drizzle with salsa, lay a quarter of the avocado slices on top, and sprinkle cilantro over all. Roll up the tortillas to enclose the filling and serve immediately.

Serves 4

Calories: 322   Total fat: 12 g   Protein: 23 g
Carbohydrates: 31 g   Cholesterol: 0 g   Sodium: 117 mg

Tex-Mex Tempeh Tacos

Serve these with crisp greens tossed with minced scallions, sliced avocado, and lime vinaigrette.

4 teaspoons light sesame oil

1 8-ounce package tempeh

1 large onion, chopped fine

4 large cloves garlic, minced

2 medium green or red bell peppers, chopped fine

1 teaspoon chili powder

1 teaspoon ground cumin

½ teaspoon ground coriander

½ teaspoon minced fresh Mexican oregano

4 plum tomatoes, peeled (page 151) and chopped

Freshly ground black pepper to taste

Salt to taste

4 large flour tortillas, warmed (see preceding recipe)

2 tablespoons chopped fresh cilantro

¼ cup grated Monterey Jack cheese (optional)

Red or green salsa to taste

Set a wok over medium heat. Add 2 teaspoons oil and swirl it to coat the bottom of the pan. Add the tempeh, turning it to coat both sides with oil. Brown well, turning occasionally. Remove the tempeh from the pan, cool somewhat, and then crumble.

Set the wok over medium-high heat. Pour in the remaining 2 teaspoons oil and swirl it to coat the pan. Add the onion and stir-fry for 2 to 3 minutes, until translucent. Add the garlic and bell pepper and continue to stir-fry for about 3 minutes. Add the chili powder, cumin, coriander, and oregano; stir-fry briefly. Stir in the tomatoes and simmer for several minutes, until saucy. Grind in black pepper and add the tempeh. Heat thoroughly, stirring often. Season with salt and remove from the heat.

Spoon the tempeh mixture onto the tortillas and garnish with the cilantro and cheese if desired. Spoon on some salsa. Fold or roll the tortillas around the filling and serve immediately.

Serves 4

Calories: 279   Total fat: 9 g   Protein: 12 g
Carbohydrates: 33 g   Cholesterol: 0 g   Sodium: 121 mg

Tempeh Tacos Too

The filling for these tacos is a Oaxacan-style picadillo, which combines finely chopped vegetables, raisins, almonds, and sweet spices with tempeh rather than the traditional ground beef or pork.

5 teaspoons peanut oil
1 8-ounce package tempeh
1 medium to large onion, chopped fine
2 large cloves garlic, minced
1 medium green bell pepper, chopped fine
Freshly ground black pepper to taste
¼ teaspoon ground cinnamon
⅛ teaspoon ground cloves
8 plum tomatoes, peeled (page 151) and
    chopped
½ teaspoon salt, plus more to taste
¼ cup raisins
1 tablespoon apple cider vinegar
¼ cup chopped lightly toasted almonds
8 small corn or 4 large flour tortillas,
    warmed (page 138)
Red or green salsa to taste

Set a wok over medium heat. Add 2 teaspoons of the oil and the tempeh. Turn the tempeh immediately to coat both sides with oil, then brown it well, turning occasionally. Remove the tempeh from the pan and chop or crumble.

Set the wok over high heat and pour the remaining tablespoon of oil around the rim. Swirl it to coat the sides of the pan. Add the onion and stir-fry for about 2 minutes, until translucent. Add the garlic and bell pepper and continue to stir-fry for 2 to 3 minutes. Add black pepper and the cinnamon and cloves; stir-fry briefly.

Stir in the tomatoes and ½ teaspoon salt. Bring to a simmer, then reduce the heat and simmer gently. Add the raisins and tempeh and cook, stirring often, for about 10 minutes.

Add the vinegar, almonds, and more black pepper and salt to taste. Spoon the mixture onto the tortillas and fold or roll them. Serve immediately, topped with salsa to taste.

Serves 4

Calories: 422   Total fat: 15 g   Protein: 16 g
Carbohydrates: 52 g   Cholesterol: 0 g   Sodium: 285 mg

Chock-Full Chapatis

Serve these spicy tofu- and vegetable-stuffed flat breads as part of your next Indian-style repast. Nectarine Ketchup (page 135) or any of the chutneys in Chapter 8 make tasty toppings.

2 teaspoons light sesame oil

½ teaspoon black mustard seeds

1 medium onion, chopped fine

4 cloves garlic, minced

1 teaspoon grated peeled fresh ginger

1 medium carrot, sliced thin or diced fine

2 medium potatoes, peeled if desired and diced fine

Pinch of cayenne or to taste

1 teaspoon ground cumin

½ teaspoon ground turmeric

¼ teaspoon ground coriander

½ pound soft or medium-firm tofu, diced

6 tablespoons vegetable stock

½ teaspoon salt, plus more to taste

1 teaspoon fresh lemon juice

Freshly ground black pepper to taste

¼ cup chopped fresh cilantro

4 to 8 flour tortillas, warmed (page 138)

Set a wok over medium-high heat. Pour the oil around the rim and swirl it to coat the pan. Sprinkle in the black mustard seeds and heat for about a minute, until they begin to pop. Add the onion and stir-fry for 2 to 3 minutes, until translucent. Continue to stir-fry for several minutes, gradually adding the garlic, ginger, carrot, and potatoes. Add the cayenne, cumin, turmeric, and coriander; stir constantly for about 1 minute, taking care not to burn the spices.

Stir in the tofu, then add the stock and ½ teaspoon salt. Cover the wok, reduce the heat slightly, and cook for 5 to 10 minutes, until the vegetables are thoroughly tender.

Add the lemon juice and black pepper. Taste and add more salt if needed. Stir in the cilantro. Fill the warm tortillas, roll them up, and serve.

Serves 4

Calories: 258	Total fat: 7 g	Protein: 8 g
Carbohydrates: 39 g	Cholesterol: 0 g	Sodium: 447 mg

Mushroom-Stuffed Steamed Buns

Here are stuffed steamed buns, Italian style. With a two-tiered bamboo rack you can steam them all at once.

1 tablespoon extra-virgin olive oil
1 medium onion, chopped fine
4 large cloves garlic, minced
¼ pound cremini or white button
    mushrooms, chopped fine
¼ pound portobello mushrooms,
    chopped fine
Freshly ground black pepper to taste
½ teaspoon minced fresh thyme **or**
    ¼ teaspoon dried
¼ teaspoon minced fresh rosemary **or** *a*
    pinch of dried
1½ tablespoons minced fresh parsley
Salt to taste
1½ pounds yeasted bread dough

Set a wok over medium-high heat. Pour the oil around the rim and swirl it to coat the pan. Add the onion and stir-fry for 2 to 3 minutes, until translucent. Add the garlic and stir-fry for 1 minute. Gradually add the mushrooms, stirring constantly. Add the pepper, thyme, and rosemary and stir-fry for about 3 minutes longer, until the mushrooms are moist and tender. Remove

the pan from the heat and add the parsley and salt to taste.

Divide the dough into eight equal pieces and form them into balls. Cover with a damp towel and let the dough relax for several minutes. Roll the balls into 4- to 5-inch disks.

Hold a disk in the palm of one hand and spoon one-eighth of the filling into the center. Pleat the edge of the circle and pinch it firmly shut. Place each bun, pinched side down, on a square of baking parchment or lightly oiled wax paper. Set the buns on a baking sheet, cover with a damp towel, and let them rise for 30 to 60 minutes, until just about doubled.

Place a steaming rack in a wok. Add water to within about an inch of the rack. Bring the water just to a simmer. Carefully arrange the risen buns on the rack. Cover the wok and steam 20 to 25 minutes, until the buns are thoroughly cooked. Serve warm.

Makes 8 buns

Calories: 195   Total fat: 5 g   Protein: 10 g
Carbohydrates: 30 g   Cholesterol: 0 g   Sodium: 453 mg

Delectable Dumplings

Use your wok to prepare the filling, then cook the dumplings.

1 8-ounce package tempeh

1 teaspoon plus 1 tablespoon light sesame oil

2 small scallions, chopped fine

2 cloves garlic, minced

1 teaspoon grated peeled fresh ginger

½ cup grated carrot

4 teaspoons shoyu or natural soy sauce or more to taste

1 tablespoon dry sherry

½ cup minced fresh cilantro

1 package (about 50) 3-inch square wonton wrappers

½ cup vegetable stock

Dumpling Dipping Sauce (page 136) or Nectarine Ketchup (page 135)

To prepare the filling, steam the tempeh over boiling water for 20 minutes. Place it in a bowl and mash thoroughly.

Add 1 teaspoon of the oil to a wok over medium heat. Add the scallions, garlic, ginger, and carrot and stir-fry for about 1 minute. Remove the wok from the heat and add the mixture to the tempeh. Add the shoyu, sherry, and cilantro; mix well.

Hold a wonton wrapper in the palm of your hand with one corner pointing downward; wet the two bottom edges of the square. Spoon about 1 teaspoon of the tempeh mixture onto the square toward the downward point. Fold the top point over the bottom one and press the edges together to seal them, forming a triangle and enclosing the filling. Wet the front of the point to your right and the back of the one to your left, then twist to bring them together and press to seal. Repeat with the remaining wrappers.

Set a wok over medium-high heat. Add the remaining tablespoon of sesame oil and swirl it to coat the pan. Add the dumplings and cook, shaking the pan periodically to keep them from sticking, until they're golden brown on both sides. Add the stock and cover the wok. Steam just until the liquid cooks away. Serve immediately with Dumpling Dipping Sauce or Nectarine Ketchup.

Serves 4 generously

Calories: 459	Total fat: 11 g	Protein: 18 g
Carbohydrates: 67 g	Cholesterol: 0 g	Sodium: 1781 mg

Indonesian Peanutty Pockets

For a bit more substance, stuff in some diced hard-cooked eggs or cooked seasoned tempeh or tofu dice. Vary the vegetables as you like and add more raw ones, too.

½ to 1 cup vegetable stock or water
1 cup thinly sliced carrot
1 cup small cauliflower florets
1 cup thinly sliced cabbage
1 cup broccoli, cut into small florets and
    thinly sliced stems
4 scallions, sliced thin
4 pitas, warmed and cut in half
4 cups well-rinsed coarsely chopped
    spinach leaves
1 cup Spicy Peanut Sauce (page 132)

Set a wok over high heat. Add ½ cup stock and bring it to a boil. Add the carrot and stir-fry, gradually adding the cauliflower, cabbage, broccoli, and more stock as needed until the vegetables are tender. Add the scallions and stir-fry briefly.

Stuff the pitas with the spinach and stir-fried vegetables and drizzle in Spicy Peanut Sauce to taste. Serve immediately.

Serves 4

Per serving with sauce:
Calories: 386   Total fat: 17 g   Protein: 14 g
Carbohydrates: 42 g   Cholesterol: 0 g   Sodium: 555 mg

Vietnamese Vegetable and Noodle Roll-Ups

Delicately spiced stir-fried vegetables and lemongrass-infused fine rice noodles rolled up in large chapatis or flour tortillas make a scrumptious snack or light lunch.

6 cups water
1 4- to 5-inch piece fresh lemongrass, sliced
3½-ounce bundle thin rice noodles
1 tablespoon peanut oil
½ cup thinly sliced scallion
2 large cloves garlic, minced
½ cup thinly sliced carrot
½ cup thinly sliced turnip
1 cup small cauliflower florets
1 teaspoon grated peeled fresh ginger
4 ounces tofu, well pressed (page 151) and
    cut into strips
1 teaspoon hot chile oil
2 to 3 tablespoons shoyu or natural soy
    sauce
1 to 2 tablespoons lime juice
½ cup chopped fresh cilantro
4 large chapatis or flour tortillas, warmed
    (page 138)

Bring the water to a boil in a large saucepan. Add the lemongrass, cover, and simmer for 10 to 15 minutes, until its flavor permeates the water. Remove from the heat and discard the lemongrass. Add the noodles to the hot water and soak for about 10 minutes, until tender but not mushy, then drain well. Cut into shorter lengths if desired.

Set a wok over high heat. Pour the oil around the rim and swirl to coat the pan. Add the scallion and garlic and stir-fry for about 1 minute. Continue stir-frying, gradually adding the carrot, turnip, cauliflower, ginger, and tofu.

When the vegetables are tender, add the chile oil, noodles, 2 tablespoons shoyu, and 1 tablespoon lime juice; toss well. Taste and add more shoyu and lime juice if needed. Mix in the cilantro. Divide among the flat breads, roll up, and serve.

Serves 4

| Calories: 258 | Total fat: 7 g | Protein: 5 g |
| Carbohydrates: 42 g | Cholesterol: 0 g | Sodium: 519 mg |

Mandarin Tortillas

Use this tasty stir-fried filling to stuff Mandarin pancakes, flour tortillas, or chapatis.

¼ cup shoyu or natural soy sauce
1 teaspoon hot chile oil
½ pound tofu, pressed (page 151) and
    diced
1 teaspoon kuzu powder
2 teaspoons cold vegetable stock or water
1½ to 2 tablespoons peanut or light
    sesame oil
2 eggs, lightly beaten
1 cup thinly sliced carrot
4 large cloves garlic, minced
1 cup slivered daikon radish
8 fresh shiitake mushrooms, stemmed and
    sliced thin
2 teaspoons minced peeled fresh ginger
4 large scallions, sliced thin
4 cups thinly sliced Chinese cabbage
¼ cup dry sherry or rice wine
½ cup chopped fresh cilantro
4 large flour tortillas, warmed (page 138)

Combine 2 tablespoons of the shoyu with the chile oil in a shallow bowl. Add the tofu and stir gently to coat. Set it aside, stirring occasionally.

Combine the kuzu, stock, and the remaining shoyu in a small bowl and set aside until the kuzu is thoroughly dissolved, about 2 minutes.

Set a wok over medium heat. Pour 1 tablespoon of the oil around the rim and swirl it to coat the pan. Add the egg and tilt the wok to spread it over the sides. When the egg is cooked on top and lightly browned on the bottom, roll it up and transfer to a cutting board. Slice it crosswise into thin strips.

Add more of the oil to the wok as needed. Add the carrot and stir-fry, gradually adding the garlic, daikon, mushrooms, ginger, and scallions. When these vegetables are tender, add the cabbage, marinated tofu, and sherry and continue stir-frying for 3 to 4 minutes. Add the dissolved kuzu mixture, shredded egg, and cilantro and stir-fry briefly. Remove from the heat.

Spoon some of the stir-fried mixture down the center of each tortilla. Roll up and serve immediately.

Serves 4

Calories: 256   Total fat: 11 g   Protein: 11 g
Carbohydrates: 20 g Cholesterol: 107 g Sodium: 1090 mg

COOKING NOTES

COOKING DRIED BEANS

A number of recipes call for cooked beans, peas, or lentils. Cooking dried beans from scratch requires some time but little effort and is much more economical than buying them precooked. You can cook beans in advance—they will keep well for 3 to 4 days in the refrigerator—or freeze extra to use for up to 4 months.

Some high-quality canned beans are available in natural foods stores and in the health food sections of some regular supermarkets, and these are convenient when you are pressed for time. Choose canned beans without preservatives and additives. Recipes in *Stir Crazy!* assume cooked beans and other legumes are unsalted, so drain and rinse canned ones to remove excess salt.

Before cooking dried beans, sort them on a tray or baking sheet and discard any shriveled, discolored specimens plus stones or other foreign matter. Rinse the picked-over beans in cool water to remove dust.

Beans are an excellent plant source of protein, iron, B vitamins, and fiber, but their good reputation is marred somewhat by the digestive discomfort they cause some people. There are several ways to minimize the flatulence that can result from certain carbohydrates in beans. First, soak the beans for several hours or overnight in 3 to 4 times as much water as beans, then pour off the soaking water and add fresh water for cooking. Besides diminishing gastric distress, soaking reduces cooking time and also helps beans hold their shape by keeping the skins from bursting before the beans are tender. Use cold water for soaking and place the pot in a cool spot (in the refrigerator in hot weather) to prevent fermentation. To expedite soaking, bring beans to a rolling boil in a covered pot for about 2 minutes, then soak them for 1 to 2 hours. Add a bay leaf or about 2 teaspoons dry epazote, an herb native to Central and South America, to the cooking water. Or add a 3-inch strip of kombu to soaking and/or cooking beans. Kombu is also a natural flavor enhancer, and it adds minerals.

Gently simmer beans to keep the skins intact, and make sure they are covered with water while cooking. Leave the pot lid slightly ajar to prevent them from boiling over. Cooking time varies with bean variety and age. Higher altitudes require longer cooking. Most beans can be cooked in a pressure cooker, and this is a convenient way to speed cooking. Follow the directions from the manufacturer for your particular pressure cooker.

Don't add salt or salty ingredients to beans until they are tender—or they may remain tough and chewy. Acidic ingredients such as lemon juice, vinegar, and mustard also hamper tenderizing. Refer to the following chart for cooking specific beans.

Bean (1 cup)	Soak	Method	Water	Time	Yield
Adzuki	Yes	Simmer, Pressure cook	4 cups 2½ to 3 cups	About 1 hour 30 minutes	2½ cups
Anasazi or Pinto	Yes	Simmer, Pressure cook	3 cups 2½ to 3 cups	2 to 2½ hours 1 hour	About 3 cups
Black-Eyed Peas	Yes	Simmer, Pressure cook	3 cups 2½ cups	1 hour 40 minutes	2½ cups
Black Turtle	Yes	Simmer, Pressure cooking not advisable	4 cups	2 to 3 hours	3 cups
Garbanzos (Chickpeas)	Yes	Simmer, Pressure cook	4 cups 2½ to 3 cups	2 to 3 hours 1 hour	3 cups
Kidney or Cannellini	Yes	Simmer, Pressure cook	3 cups 2½ cups	1 to 1½ hours 45 minutes	3 cups
Lentils (green or brown)	No	Simmer, Pressure cook	2 to 3 cups 2½ cups	45 minutes 25 minutes	3 cups
Mung	No	Simmer, Pressure cook	3 cups 2½ cups	45 minutes 25 minutes	3 cups
Navy (Pea)	Yes	Simmer, Pressure cook	3 cups 2½ cups	1 to 1½ hours 40 minutes	2½ to 3 cups
Split Peas	No	Simmer, Pressure cook	3 cups 2½ cups	45 to 60 minutes 20 minutes	2 cups

COOKING GRAINS

Most packaged grains are quite clean, but bulk grains may have some small twigs or stones in their midst. Spread suspect grain in a single layer on a tray or baking sheet and check carefully for inedible particles. After measuring, rinse raw whole grains thoroughly. I do this by swirling the grain in a bowl of cool water in the sink and then pouring off the water and any harvest debris that floats to the top. Repeat this process several times until the water is clear, then drain the grain well in a fine-mesh strainer.

Coordinate pot size and the quantity of grain to be cooked. Grains require sufficient room to expand, but a small amount in a large pot won't cook evenly and thoroughly no matter how long it simmers. Use a 1- to 2-quart pot for a cup of dry grain. By the way, when increasing the quantity of grain, you won't need to increase the liquid absolutely proportionately. For instance, use 1¾ to 2 cups of water for 1 cup of rice and 3 cups of water for 2 cups rice.

Grains cook most efficiently in relatively heavy, well-insulated pots with tight-fitting lids. Place the rinsed, drained grain in the pot, then add a pinch of salt and the measured liquid. Bring it to a boil, stir once, cover the pot tightly, and reduce the heat as low as possible; I set the pot on a flame tamer (radiant heat diffuser) for exceptionally low, even heat. Cook the grain for the amount of time specified in the chart. Grains continue cooking after the heat is turned off, so leave the pot covered for at least 10 minutes while the grain finishes steaming.

Grain (1 cup)	Water	Cooking Time	Yield
Barley	3 cups	1 to 1½ hours	3½ to 4 cups
Buckwheat	1½ cups	15 minutes	3 to 4 cups
Bulgur	1½ cups	15 minutes	3 cups
Couscous	1½ cups	Soak 10 minutes	3 cups
Jasmine Rice	2 cups	20 minutes	3 to 4 cups
Millet	2 cups	20 minutes	4 cups
Quinoa	1½ cups	15 minutes	4 cups
Rice (Long-grain brown or brown basmati)	1¾ cups	40 minutes	3 to 4 cups
Wild Rice	1¾ cups	40 minutes	3 to 4 cups

PEELING TOMATOES, PEACHES, OR NECTARINES

Bring a pot of water to a rapid boil. Briefly immerse the tomatoes, peaches, or nectarines in the boiling water, then transfer them to a container of cold water. The skin will slip off readily.

SPECIAL TOFU TECHNIQUES

Pressing Tofu

Tofu is often pressed to make it firmer and increase its ability to absorb flavorings. To press a block of tofu, sandwich it between paper or unnapped cloth towels on a baking sheet or flat tray. Then place a second sheet or cutting board over it with a weight of some kind—cans, a pan of water, or the like—on top of that. I often press a single block in one of those small plastic baskets that cherry tomatoes and berries come in; my square marble paperweight fits perfectly on top. You can also press tofu in a colander or strainer with a plate and weight on top.

Freezing Tofu

Freezing and thawing tofu gives it a spongy, chewy chickenlike texture and renders it superabsorbent. Drain a block of firm tofu, seal it in a plastic container or freezer bag, and freeze for 24 hours to 6 months. Thaw the tofu completely in the refrigerator.

Blanching or Steaming Tofu

It's a good idea to blanch (parboil) or steam tofu (except for freshly made or silken tofu) that you plan to eat uncooked—marinated, mashed, or puréed. Brief blanching or steaming freshens tofu's flavor, improves digestibility, and wards off bacteria that may develop during storage. These processes also firm tofu slightly and increase its absorbency. To blanch, place whole, sliced, or cubed tofu in boiling water for up to 5 minutes; remove it with a slotted spoon and drain well. Steam tofu in a steamer or on a rack in a regular pot over gently boiling water for the same length of time. In either case, the tofu will soften and remain somewhat fragile until it cools.

GLOSSARY

Achiote seeds These hard brick-red seeds come from the South American evergreen annatto tree. Sautéed in oil, then removed, their subtle taste and intense yellow-orange hue will pervade an entire dish.

Adzuki (Aduki or Azuki) beans These small round dark red beans are traditionally featured in Japanese cuisine. Particularly low in fat, they have a subtly sweet flavor and are especially easy to digest.

Anasazi beans The unhybridized ancestors of pinto beans, anasazi beans resemble them in size and shape but are maroon with white splotches when raw. They have a fuller, sweeter flavor than pintos, hold their shape better when cooked, and are also easier to digest.

Arborio rice This exceptionally starchy short-grain rice is customarily used for the classic northern Italian dish risotto. Each small grain softens and swells as it absorbs considerable hot liquid, creating a creamy yet still slightly firm-to-the-bite texture.

Arrowroot A starchy root named for its use in drawing poison from arrow wounds in its native West Indies, arrowroot is used in a dried, powdered form primarily as a thickener. Dissolve it in cold water before adding it to a hot liquid. Arrowroot is virtually tasteless and gives sauces a clear, glazed appearance. Its thickening power has limited duration and tends to break down upon reheating.

Balsamic vinegar This dark amber-colored Italian vinegar is aged in wooden barrels for at least three years. It has a somewhat thick, syrupy consistency and a sweet-sour flavor.

Bulgur This nutty-flavored, quick-cooking grain is prepared by parboiling or steaming wheat berries, then drying and cracking them. Available in different degrees of coarseness, bulgur is used extensively in Middle Eastern cuisines.

Capers The pickled flower buds of a Mediterranean shrub, these small green spheres add punch to sauces and other preparations. My favorite kind are packed dry in coarse salt rather than bottled in a briny solution; rinse them before use.

Celeriac (celery root) This large round rootlike vegetable is a close relative of familiar stalk celery and has a similar flavor. It is tasty both raw and cooked. Select relatively small celeriac, because a large one is likely to have a spongy center. Celeriac's uneven surface, beset with hairy roots, is tricky to clean and best peeled away. Submerge raw slices in cold lemon water to keep them from turning brown.

Chestnuts, dried Look for these at natural foods stores or gourmet shops. Low in fat, and mostly monounsaturated fat at that, chestnuts have a starchy, nonoily texture.

Coconut milk This luscious liquid is the secret ingredient in many Southeast Asian dishes. Look for canned commercial coconut milk—without additives and preservatives—at Asian markets and natural foods stores. To make your own, combine equal amounts of grated fresh coconut with hot water in a blender or food processor. Blend well and then set aside for about 30 minutes. Strain, pressing out as much liquid as possible. A cup each of coconut and water will produce about 1 cup of coconut milk. Use 1½ cups hot water to 1 cup of dried unsweetened coconut.

Couscous You'll find both whole wheat and refined couscous made from durum wheat that is formed into fine strands, then dried and cracked into tiny pieces. Though traditionally steamed over a stew or soup in its native North Africa, this light fluffy grain requires only soaking in boiling liquid.

Cremini mushrooms Also called *Italian brown mushrooms,* these are cousins to common white button mushrooms but have a fuller flavor and slightly firmer texture.

Daikon radish The flavor of this long white icicle-shaped radish has a bite when raw and becomes sweet when cooked. It is thought to facilitate the digestion of oils.

Fava beans Sometimes called *broad beans,* large oval fava beans are enclosed in giant green pods when fresh. Peel off the thick outer skin of individual beans because it may taste bitter. Soak light brown dried favas and then remove their leatherlike skin before cooking. Cooked fava beans have a somewhat nutty flavor and a delicious soft, smooth texture.

Garbanzo beans Also known as *chickpeas,* these lumpy round beige beans are often featured in Middle Eastern, Mediterranean, and Indian cuisines. Rich in iron, calcium, and protein, they have a hearty, nutty flavor and retain their shape when cooked.

Gumbo filé This traditional seasoning in classic Creole gumbos is prepared from ground dried young sassafras leaves. Do not boil a mixture after adding filé powder, or its texture may become unpleasantly stringy.

Hot chile oil Used as a flavoring in Asian dishes, this is oil infused with hot pepper seeds. Buy it prepared or make your own by adding dried red pepper seeds to heated light sesame or peanut oil. Strain the oil when its flavor reaches a desired hotness and refrigerate it to retard rancidity.

Jalapeño chiles Small and relatively narrow with a rounded end and thick, dark green to bright red skin, these chiles are flavorful and moderately hot. Remove some or all of the seeds and veins to modulate their heat.

Jasmine rice Traditionally cultivated in Thailand, this exceedingly aromatic rice has a delicate nutty flavor and somewhat sticky texture.

Jícama This large brown bulbous underground tuber from Central America has a somewhat sweet flavor and crisp, moist flesh something like a water chestnut or Jerusalem artichoke. Peel and serve this vegetable raw or cooked; it retains its firm texture when cooked.

Kalamata (calamata) olives These large purplish black Greek olives have a full, briny flavor. Look for them pitted for convenience.

Kohlrabi This early spring turnip-shaped vegetable is a member of the cabbage family. It has a mild broccoli flavor and crisp texture. Peel off its thick green or purple skin and julienne it for salads or add it to stir-fries.

Kombu This nutrient-rich sea vegetable contains the natural flavor enhancer glutamic acid. Add a strip of dark green dried kombu to soup stock and cook it with dried beans to increase their digestibility.

Kuzu *Kudzu* in the United States, this is the powdered root of a vine indigenous to Japan that's renowned for its medicinal properties and excellence as a thickener and gelling agent. A white, tasteless starch, it produces transparent sauces and glazes. Dissolve kuzu in a cold liquid before adding it to the hot one you're thickening. Kuzu comes in a chunky form. Mash or grind it to make measuring more accurate and dissolving quicker.

Lemongrass This tropical reedlike herb is a common ingredient in Thai and other Southeast Asian cuisines. Peel off the tough outer layer of stalk and mince the tender core; it gives dishes a gentle lemony flavor. Steeped fresh or dried lemongrass leaves make a refreshing tea or stock.

Lemon thyme One of many thyme varieties, this has a tangy lemony undertone.

Marsala Originally from Marsala, Sicily, this sweet-flavored dessert wine enhances certain savory dishes too.

Mexican oregano Not a true oregano, this relative has a similar, though more intense, zesty flavor.

Millet This gluten-free grain, native to India and Africa, looks like tiny golden spheres. It has a delicate, slightly nutty flavor that's enhanced by dry-roasting before cooking. Millet's alkaline nature makes it especially digestible.

Mirin This is a sweet Japanese rice wine with a low alcohol content, prepared by fermenting sweet brown rice, water, and rice koji, a cultured grain starter. Mirin balances flavors in soy-based sauces.

Miso Fermented soybean paste, miso is composed of cooked soybeans, salt, water, a grain culture (called *koji*) and sometimes cooked rice, barley, or another grain. Depending on the type of miso, it's aged from two months to three years. A good source of protein and digestive enzymes, miso serves as a salt substitute but also contributes a unique flavor dimension to soups, stews, sauces, and other dishes. For best flavor and most nutrients, look for unpasteurized misos, containing beneficial bacteria and active enzymes; to preserve these, take care not to boil mixtures after adding miso. Store miso in the refrigerator, where it will keep indefinitely.

Mung beans These small round army-green beans cook quickly without presoaking. Sprouted, they add a gentle crunch—and extra vitamins—to Asian-style stir-fries.

Oyster mushrooms These delicate light gray fan-shaped mushrooms grow on tree limbs and trunks. They require minimal cooking and have a subtle, slightly nutty or oysterlike flavor and luscious texture. Go easy on oil and seasonings to let them shine.

Porcini This is the Italian name for wild woodland forest mushrooms; they are also called *cèpes*. These light brown mushrooms have large flat caps, stubby stems, and a spongy underside rather than gills. Available both fresh and dried, their flavor is rich and assertive.

Portobello mushrooms Giant cousins to cremini and white button mushrooms, these may grow to 10 inches in diameter. They have an exceptionally meaty texture and wonderfully rich flavor, particularly when broiled or grilled.

Quinoa An ancient staple of the Inca tribes in South America, this light, nutty-flavored, quick-cooking grainlike food (technically it's the fruit of an herb) is making a comeback. Gluten-free and exceptionally rich in high-quality protein, quinoa also contains abundant vitamins and minerals. Rinse it well before cooking to wash off any lingering saponin, a bitter-tasting natural coating that protects the plant from insects.

Rau ram Also called *Vietnamese coriander,* this Asian herb tastes much like cilantro with a lemony undertone.

Rice noodles You'll find a large selection of rice noodles, or "rice sticks," at Asian markets and some supermarkets, natural foods stores, and gourmet shops. Most are brittle and ivory colored. Depending on thickness, they cook in 1 to 5 minutes, or soak them in hot water for about 15 minutes and then stir-fry. Follow directions on the package.

Saffron The dried stamens of a southern European crocus, saffron contributes a rich golden color and its unique flavor to rice and other preparations. Fortunately, a little bit of saffron goes a long way, because a single pound of this precious spice requires 70,000 to 80,000 flowers.

Shiitake mushrooms These light grayish-brown, large-capped mushrooms are available both fresh and dried. They're prized for their full flavor, tender texture, and healing properties. Add their tough stems to your stockpot.

Shoyu This is the Japanese term for traditionally made soy sauce consisting of soybeans, wheat, salt, and water that's naturally fermented and aged for one to two years. Add shoyu near the end of cooking to preserve its flavor.

Soba These thin Japanese noodles contain either all buckwheat flour or some combination of buckwheat and whole or refined wheat flour. Other substances, such as powdered mugwort or wild yam, are sometimes included for flavor variations and extra nutrients. For cooking directions, see page 115.

Soy milk At its most basic, this is prepared by blending ground cooked soybeans with water and then straining the "milky" liquid. It contains no lactose or cholesterol and is low in saturated fats. A large variety of commercial soy milks are readily available, most commonly in aseptic packaging. Select plain unsweetened soymilk for cooking.

Sucanat Short for *sugar cane natural,* this is the trademark name for evaporated, granulated sugar cane juice (available organic). Processed without chemicals, this light brown sweetener is less refined than white sugar and retains some trace elements. Substitute it in equal amounts for standard white or brown sugar.

Tahini This smooth, creamy paste made from hulled sesame seeds is available both raw and roasted. Look for organic tahini to avoid chemical residues from pesticides and processing solvents.

Tamari Originally the liquid that separated out as all-soybean miso aged, this seasoning now refers to naturally fermented wheat-free soy sauce. Tamari has a fuller flavor than shoyu and endures better in stews and other long-cooked dishes.

Tamarind The pod of a tropical tree indigenous to east Africa and India, tamarind contains a vitamin-rich dark, sticky, tart pulp that is used as a flavoring in sauces and other preparations. For convenience, look for jarred tamarind concentrate at Asian food stores.

Udon Flat linguinelike noodles, udon are composed of whole or sifted wheat flour and sometimes part rice flour. Made of lower-gluten wheat than most Western pastas, these tender-textured Asian noodles are best prepared by the "shock" method described on page 105.

Umeboshi vinegar Though not really a vinegar, this dark red liquid, drawn off Japanese umeboshi plums after pickling, is used in the same ways. Its color comes from iron-rich shiso leaves, an herb that's packed together with the plums and sea salt during pickling. Umeboshi vinegar not only adds zest to foods, but is also a digestive aid. Just remember it tastes salty as well as sour!

Vegetable stock See page xiii.

Wild rice Not actually a grain, but the seeds of a wild grass common in marshy regions of the northern Midwest and southern Canada, wild rice is traditionally hand-harvested by Indian tribes in those areas. Because of its ever-increasing popularity, wild rice now also is cultivated, primarily in California and the northwestern United States. I like to combine wild rice with regular long-grain or basmati brown rice to tone down its especially earthy flavor and to cut down on cost.

INDEX